Carlyle and Emerson

Carlyle and Emerson
Their Long Debate

Kenneth Marc Harris

Harvard University Press
Cambridge, Massachusetts
and London, England
1978

Publication of this book has been aided by a grant from the
Andrew W. Mellon Foundation

Library of Congress Cataloging in Publication Data

Harris, Kenneth Marc, 1948-
    Carlyle and Emerson, their long debate.

    Includes bibliographical references and index.
    1. Carlyle, Thomas, 1795-1881 — Philosophy.
2. Emerson, Ralph Waldo, 1803-1882 — Philosophy.
3. Carlyle, Thomas, 1795-1881 — Correspondence.
4. Emerson, Ralph Waldo, 1803-1882 — Correspondence.
5. Authors, Scottish — Correspondence. 6. Authors, American — Correspondence. I. Title.
PR4437.P5H3   824'.8   77-28036
ISBN 0-674-09755-6

For Clare

Acknowledgments

"Much that is foolish has been said as to this acquaintance," wrote George Saintsbury of the Carlyle-Emerson friendship in his obituary for Emerson in *The Academy* (May 6, 1882). I take full responsibility for whatever nonsense might be found in this book. For whatever sense is in it, on the other hand, I feel that much of the credit should go to others, specifically, to previous students of Carlyle and of Emerson and to three of my teachers at Harvard University. Jerome Hamilton Buckley deserves my deepest gratitude for his sure advice, heartening encouragement, and meticulous correction of the manuscript. Joel Porte could always be relied on to point out any foolishness Buckley might have missed. Merely because he knew what I was working on, Daniel Aaron would often drop casual remarks that ultimately had a great impact on what I wrote; he also helped transform a part of this book into a self-contained little article. My debt to past scholars obviously cannot be expressed in personal terms, and anyway there are too many of them. But I must single out Joseph Slater, whose edition of the Carlyle-Emerson correspondence has been before me, literally and figuratively, at every stage of my work. Without his careful editing of the letters and his concise, thorough, and suggestive introduction, I would not have known where to begin (or even whether I should). Finally, the excerpts I have included from Emerson's lecture notes are published by permission of the Houghton Library, Harvard University, and the Ralph Waldo Emerson Memorial Association; I appreciate their assistance.

Contents

I have not at any time forgotten you, be that justice done the unfortunate: and tho' I see well enough what a great deep cleft divides us, in our ways of practically looking at this world, —I see also (as probably you do yourself) where the rock-strata, miles deep, unite again; and the two poor souls are at one. Poor devils!—Nay if there were no point of agreement at all, and I were more intolerant of "ways of thinking" than I even am, —yet has not the man Emerson, from old years, been a Human Friend to me? Can I ever forget, or think otherwise than lovingly of the man Emerson?

—Carlyle to Emerson, 19 July 1850

Let it be an alliance of two large, formidable natures, mutually beheld, mutually feared, before yet they recognize the deep identity which, beneath these disparities, unites them.

—Emerson, "Friendship"

Abbreviations

L   *The Correspondence of Emerson and Carlyle.* Ed. Joseph Slater. New York, 1964.

SR   Thomas Carlyle. *Sartor Resartus.* Ed. Charles F. Harrold. New York, 1937.

CW   Thomas Carlyle. *Works,* centenary edition, ed. H. D. Traill. 30 vols. London, 1896-1901.

EW   Ralph Waldo Emerson. *Works,* centenary edition, ed. Edward Waldo Emerson. 12 vols. Boston, 1903-1904.

NAL *Collected Works of Ralph Waldo Emerson.* Ed. Alfred R. Ferguson. Vol. I, *Nature, Addresses, and Lectures.* Cambridge, Mass., 1971.

ET   Ralph Waldo Emerson. *English Traits.* Ed. Howard Mumford Jones. Cambridge, Mass., 1966.

> *Note:* These abbreviations are used for citations of primary sources. For the sake of appearance, arabic numbers followed by a colon are used to indicate the volume numbers of multivolume works. This form is maintained only for the works listed above; for other works, traditional documentation is used.

Introduction

The state of Society in our days is, of all possible states, the least an unconscious one: this is specially the Era when all manner of Inquiries into what was once the unfelt, involuntary sphere of man's existence, find their place, and, as it were, occupy the whole domain of thought.

— CARLYLE, "CHARACTERISTICS"

The key to the period appeared to be that the mind had become aware of itself. Men grew reflective and intellectual. There was a new consciousness . . . The young men were born with knives in their brain, a tendency to introversion, self-dissection, anatomizing of motives.

— EMERSON, "HISTORIC NOTES OF LIFE AND LETTERS IN NEW ENGLAND"

When the young Carlyle characterized his era as "the least an unconscious one," and the aging Emerson recalled that same period as the birth of a universal self-awareness, they could not avoid the implication that the preceding generations had gone through life in a sort of trance. All through history, it seemed, not only had people failed to examine their thoughts and beliefs, but they had not even been aware that their thoughts might bear reflection and their beliefs might be open to question, until at last the mesmerist snapped his fingers and the human mind gained "consciousness." Carlyle and Emerson tried to soften the insult to their ancestors' intelligence by insisting that it was spiritually healthier to have faith without reflection — to live in a trance — than to be born with a knife in one's brain, provided the somnambulist remained unaware of his condition. But their own eyes had been opened, whether or not they were better off for it. They preferred to regard their fathers' beliefs as free from self-consciousness rather than as contingent on self-delusion, so that they could maintain a certain piety as they turned their backs on their spiritual inheritance.

They had abandoned the old religion, they said, not because it was false but because they lacked the "unconscious" state of mind which would have enabled them to believe. Not to fall into skepticism and materialism was for both a point of honor, but there seemed to be no escape. They were imprisoned by their own self-awareness. How could they consciously will themselves to "lose consciousness" and thereby attain faith? They could not remove the knives from their brains.

A crucial element in their resolution of the dilemma was the conjecture of a dual mode of thought, both "conscious" and "unconscious" at the same time. The distinction was metaphysical as well as psychological, for they hoped to assimilate the supernatural truths that their parents accepted without reflection through the unreflective portion of the mind, all the while retaining the critical, self-dissecting qualities of intellect which otherwise would render such beliefs incredible. To put it another way, they hoped to dream with their eyes open. It was a very neat stratagem, and the fact that it really did not make much sense actually increased its attractiveness to them, because Carlyle and Emerson had in common a strain of irrationality. Henry James pointed out this shared trait shortly after their deaths, although he was quick to contrast the mental aberrations of Emerson, which were "mild as moonlight," with the near psychopathy of Carlyle, who was "like a man hovering on the edge of insanity—hanging over a black gulf and wearing the reflection of its bottomless deeps in his face."[1]

James may have exaggerated the distance between the two men, but he shrewdly perceived the underlying similarity. It was primarily Carlyle's fascination with the irrational and the "unconscious" (a term he was one of the first to use) in such early works as "Characteristics" that drove Emerson to seek out the obscure young author in the hinterlands of Scotland. And it was Emerson's youthful eagerness to explore realms of thought beyond the limits of reason that made the unexpected visit from a self-defrocked American clergyman such an eternally memorable experience for Carlyle. In the irrational depths of their own minds there was a profound identity between them. Perhaps this was what Carlyle meant when he wrote to Emerson many years later that despite the "great deep cleft" that divided them in their "ways of practically looking at this world," he still believed that "the rock-strata, miles deep, unite again; and the two poor souls are at one" (L, p. 459). The cleft was visible almost from the first, and throughout their lives it grew deeper and wider. But in a sense the cleft only serves to reveal the fundamental solidity of the bedrock.

In less subterranean matters the two men had little in common. Both started out in life with the intention of entering the ministry and both became professional men of letters. The parallel could be stretched a little further by adding that both were from "old Puritan stock," but Emerson was raised as a Unitarian and preached for a while from a Unitarian pulpit, whereas the Carlyle family belonged to an austere Calvinist sect and Carlyle's own ecclesiastical career never went beyond a couple of practice sermons. The differences, in any case, are far more pronounced. Carlyle was the son of a peasant, but he lived more than half his life in Lon-

don. Emerson was a city boy who made his home in rural
Concord, where he became a gentleman farmer and raised a
family with his unassuming second wife, Lidian (originally
"Lydia," a name he disliked). Carlyle's wife, Jane Welsh,
possessed both a literary endowment and an often disagree-
able personality nearly equal to her husband's; they endured
a long, often stormy marriage which was childless (and possibly sexless). Both men lived to a senile old age. Emerson,
when he was young, thought he had contracted the family
scourge, lung disease, but when he was turning seventy he
told Charles Eliot Norton that he did not know what it was
to be ill for a whole day. The same thing was said of Carlyle
by his friend and biographer, James Anthony Froude, but
Carlyle himself, Froude added, never admitted that he ever
felt well.[2] Emerson was certainly easier to get along with
than Carlyle; he had an amiable, pacific nature. Carlyle,
however, must have been a more interesting person to meet;
he was famous for his wild conversation and his hearty
laugh. But they were both difficult people to get to know. I
do not believe anyone ever claimed to have been really close
to either of them.

It is hard to say how close they were to each other. All the
days in which they came face to face during Emerson's three
trips to Europe probably amounted to no more than a
month. Yet they shared the most important events of their
mature years through their letters. Now their relationship
seems in some ways like a disembodied meeting of minds,
but at many points — at moments of crisis, or when a death
occurs — the two lives touch intimately. If has often been
speculated that if they had lived near each other their
friendship would never have lasted. That may be true. They
had other good friends with whom they were better acquainted personally. Emerson had Thoreau, who somewhat
resembled Carlyle in his impatience with cant and in his love
of argument. Emerson's memorial speech for Thoreau is
strikingly similar to his memorial speech for Carlyle, although he never made the comparison himself.[3] Carlyle had

John Sterling, who along with Emerson was among the very small number of people who could contradict Carlyle and still retain his respect. I do not mean to suggest that Carlyle and Emerson might have been friendly neighbors after all, or that Sterling and Thoreau knew Carlyle and Emerson better than the two older men knew each other. Such matters cannot be determined. What can be said is that because they communicated almost exclusively through letters, and because those letters are so remarkable in themselves, a record exists of their relationship that is as extensive and as significant as the record of either man's relationship with anyone else. In other words, so far as we know, they were the best of friends. And if their books are read, as I like to read them, in conjunction with their letters as the public continuation of a private dialogue which lasted almost forty years, then it could be said that the record of their association is as complete as that of any other friendship in history.

One reason why their relationship was so successful was that it got off to such a warm start. Aside from the intellectual and spiritual interests they shared when they were young, at the time of their first meeting each was suffering from a recent bereavement, and there was probably a mutual exchange of personal sympathy. Emerson had undertaken the European voyage to help him recover from the loss of his first wife, Ellen, who had died at the age of nineteen. We know that he told the Carlyles about Ellen when he stayed with them at Craigenputtock; Carlyle remembered thirty years later.[4] It is reasonable to assume that while consoling Emerson, Carlyle would have spoken of the death of his father, which occurred the previous year. For each of them, the event had been a shattering experience.[5]

Death was a lifelong preoccupation for them, perhaps another trait they held in common. When he was in his twenties, Carlyle underwent a moment of crisis which he described in *Sartor Resartus* as a victorious defiance of death and the devil. But the victory was not decisive; in later years he often reacted with violent emotion to the thought as well as to the fact of death. The theme of death is just as strong, though less obtrusive, in the life and works of Emerson.[6] Their intense personal concern is reflected in their speculative writings, for they regarded the transcendence of death as the acid test of whatever new modes of belief they hoped would arise to replace the old religion. Ernest Becker has described the history of culture as "the succession of ideologies that console for death."[7] Carlyle and Emerson were painfully conscious of living in an age when one such ideology had lost that power to console, and they desperately wanted to assist in the discovery of another.

They knew they could not do it by themselves because they were not systematic philosophers. The ideas on which they based their fancies and speculations were not their own; most of them came from German philosophy, especially from Kant and Fichte. Carlyle had more direct access to German thought than did Emerson, who probably knew little German, at least when he was young. To be sure, Carlyle also depended heavily on secondary sources, but he did try to read around in the originals, here and there, and he forcibly wrenched out whatever appealed to him, often at the cost of outrageous distortion. It is easy to belittle Carlyle's grasp of Kant, for example, but it should be remembered that he had learned German virtually on his own and that he was one of very few British readers of some very difficult works. (In the *Critique of Pure Reason,* part of which Carlyle knew directly, the German is particularly exasperating: there are pronouns with a multiplicity of possible antecedents, terms which change their gender, and interminable sentences jammed with clauses from different manuscripts.)[8] That he tried to read Kant at all is a tribute to his determination; that he found so much that he could use, however inaccurately, is a tribute to his imagination as well as his intellect. Emerson relied on Coleridge and on Carlyle himself for his understanding of German philosophy; he was also influenced by other speculative writers seldom mentioned by Carlyle, especially Swedenborg. In the discussion of Transcendentalism which follows, I have not attempted to identify the ultimate sources of their ideas; other, abler scholars have already accomplished that strenuous labor.[9] It is, as Charles Frederick Harrold said, "a hazardous task": typically, the critic presents a passage from, let us say, Carlyle, identifies the original concept in Kant or wherever, then comments on the (sometimes enormous) disparity, at the same time suggesting intermediary authors (Novalis, the Schlegels) who might also account for the distortions.

The sources of their ideas, and even in a sense the ideas themselves, are less important than the literary uses to which Carlyle and Emerson committed those ideas. They felt they lived in an age when the mind had become conscious of its own workings; yet the faith which people needed was dependent on the very absence of such self-awareness. To resolve the contradiction, they may have believed that as artists they had as much to contribute as the philosophers. Artists can embody what the philosophers merely explain, for artistic creation involves the unconscious as well as the conscious mind. Only artists and madmen dream with their eyes open — and tell us their dreams.

1

The Transatlantic Transcendentalists: "Natural Supernaturalism" and *Nature*

The talk between Carlyle and Emerson during their brief first meeting at Craigenputtock in 1833 ranged over a wide variety of topics, from the ingenuity of Carlyle's pig and the debased condition of contemporary literature to the current upsurge of rick burning by unemployed Irish immigrants and the immortality of the soul. Carlyle's thoughts on this last subject were of great interest to Emerson. In his short account of their day together in *English Traits* (1856), the exchange on immortality is carefully set off from everything else. It begins with a dramatic shift of scenery. Presumably the two men had passed the first few hours of their acquaintance inside the old farmhouse, for now they "went out to walk over long hills, and looked at Criffel, then without his cap, and down into Wordsworth's country." In other words the sky was so clear that even the summit of a distant mountain was free of clouds, and the far-sighted could see very far indeed. Emerson remembers:

> There we sat down and talked of the immortality of the soul. It was not Carlyle's fault that we talked on that topic, for he had the natural disinclination of every nimble spirit to bruise itself against walls, and did not like to place himself where no step can be taken. But he was honest and true, and cognizant of the subtile links that bind ages together, and saw how every event affects all the future. "Christ died on the tree; that built

Dunscore kirk yonder; that brought you and me together. Time has only a relative existence." (*ET*, p. 10)

After the lengthy overture, Carlyle's oracular statement sounds like a voice from the cloudless sky, or like "a Spirit addressing Spirits," as Teufelsdröckh's Editor once described himself. It is also the only direct discourse longer than a phrase to have survived from the entire visit.

There is no reason to doubt Emerson's accuracy, since he wrote down Carlyle's words in his journal soon after he heard them.[1] And from a distance of many years he may have seen in this idyllic vignette a certain poetic truth about his ultimate relation to Carlyle with respect to Transcendental speculation. But an accurate memory may still be selective, and in this case Emerson's selectivity amounts to a subtle distortion of his reaction to Carlyle at the time. Actually he was much more persistent in his efforts to corner Carlyle theologically than the immortality anecdote suggests, and he was so disappointed with Carlyle's evasions that he began to doubt Carlyle's very capacity for speculative thought. Emerson's perseverance on this subject is excusable, since he had been drawn to Carlyle in the first place largely through his more speculative writings, such as the essay "Characteristics" and the prophetic conclusion of "State of German Literature." But when he asked Carlyle about the "religious development" implicit in these particular pieces, Carlyle "replied, that he was not competent to state it even to himself"—an admission Emerson reported five days after the Craigenputtock visit in a letter to a friend in England. There is no mention in this letter of his extracting from Carlyle any intimations of immortality, only a vague remark about "all the great questions that interest us most." While strongly expressing his love for Carlyle and conceding that he was "the most catholic of philosophers," Emerson bluntly declared that he "had met with men of far less power who had yet greater insight into religious truth."[2] He must have felt that, at least in some respects, he had overestimated his

"Germanick new-light writer" (as he once referred to Carlyle before he had learned his name). Perhaps Carlyle was really no more than an amiable writer of reviews, and in praising him as a "catholic" philosopher, Emerson may have been politely condemning him as a mere appropriator of the ideas of others.

By the time Emerson wrote his first letter to Carlyle, nine months had elapsed since Craigenputtock and most of *Sartor Resartus* had appeared in *Fraser's Magazine*. Emerson had read as far as "The Everlasting No,"[3] and his letter (L, pp. 97-101) exhibits the inevitable confusion of someone in that situation. There is much light-hearted criticism of "this grotesque teutonic apocalyptic strain of yours," but through the levity it becomes apparent that Emerson's opinion of Carlyle's claims to religious insight has undergone further change. He half seriously suggests that the eccentric style is a result of Carlyle's fear that he has no readers among his contemporaries, and so Emerson reminds him of the relative existence of time. If Carlyle still believes "that it was Jesus Christ built Dunscore kirk," then he must agree that "no poet is sent into the world before his time." This allusion to their talk at Craigenputtock seems to encourage Emerson to state his objections to the new book more explicitly: "I comprehend not why you should lavish in that spendthrift style of yours Celestial truths." At Craigenputtock Carlyle had been so reticent about "Celestial truths" that Emerson suspected he did not know any. Happily, in *Sartor Resartus* he could see "that which is rarest, namely, the simplest truths," such truths, no doubt, as he had originally discerned in Carlyle's earlier essays. Only now the simple truth is not spoken plainly so that all can understand, but lies hidden, almost buried, beneath the writing.

Upon completion of his critique, Emerson immediately softens his language. "I may repent my temerity & unsay my charge," he begins; and with a foretaste of what will some day develop into a major Emersonian concept, he continues, "For are not all our circlets of will as so many little eddies rounded in by the great circle of Necessity & *could* the Truth-Speaker perhaps now the best Thinker of the Saxon race, have written otherwise?" This qualification not only attests to Emerson's sincere recognition of Carlyle's true powers, but also reveals a substantial growth in maturity and intellectual power in Emerson since his return from Europe.

But despite his concession to the "circlets of will" circumscribed by Necessity, the young Emerson still would prefer a less ambiguous revelation. "I look for the hour with impatience when the vehicle will be worthy of the spirit," he says in the letter, "when the word will be as simple & so as resistless as the thought, & in short when your words will be one with things." But to communicate new truths, or to regenerate old ones, both Carlyle and Emerson would find that making their words one with things demanded new words, almost a new language.

Emerson might have been better prepared for Carlyle's reluctance to discuss religious matters at Craigenputtock had he read "Characteristics" more carefully, for there the compulsion to describe and explain religion rather than just accept it instinctively is considered a sign of religious decay. Lamentations for the decline of religion and indictments of the present age as an era of unbelief are common themes throughout the nineteenth century; nevertheless, the nineteenth century probably exceeds all other centuries in total volume of literature examining, and usually defending, religion in one form or another. The paradox might seem to support the thesis of "Characteristics," although the obverse of Carlyle's proposition, that a drastic diminishment of such writing would necessarily indicate a healthier religious environment, is hardly borne out by twentieth-century experience.

There is an interesting variation in an unrelated source on Carlyle's theory in "Characteristics" of the self-consciousness of nineteenth-century religion. In his study of Milton, first published in 1930, E. M. W. Tillyard divided religious faith

into "scientific" and "poetic" components, tending, respectively, toward literal and allegorical (or moral) interpretations of the Bible. In earlier times, Tillyard explained, it
was possible to believe in heaven and hell and the fall of
man, for example, in both ways simultaneously without
having to "sort out the measure of scientific belief and the
measure of poetic belief" in one's mind. Carlyle would probably accept this as a description of healthy, "unconscious"
religion. But as the discoveries of modern physical science
were perceived as moving toward ever greater conflict with a
literal understanding of religious revelations, a strong polar-
izing trend set in. This polarization involves more than the
familiar split between literalists and allegorizers, which is a
far more ancient distinction among the religious, though it,
too, doubtlessly accelerated in the nineteenth century. The
new dichotomy Tillyard proposed arose from within, from
the responsibility felt by each individual to distinguish in his
own mind which elements in his beliefs he took literally and
which he regarded as "poetic." Understandably, the process
could be agonizing. "To say that you disbelieved in Adam
and Eve," Tillyard illustrated, "was of course a much worse
thing in Milton's day than in Victoria's, but to say that you
did believe was not half so exacting."[4] In Carlyle's terms,
religion had become pathologically conscious of itself.

    In "Characteristics," the imperative to describe and ana-
lyze is declared a symptom of disease not only in religion but
in all aspects of modern life. What Carlyle was attacking,
when considered as a state of mind, might also be expressed
by such catchwords as "critical spirit," "scientific attitude,"
"British empiricism," "materialism," and "rationalism." All
these connote ways of thinking which emphasize precision,
explicitness, and strict accuracy. To put it differently, this
mode of thought prizes knowledge of what is or, at least, of
what can be known and rejects speculation of what might be
or what cannot be known in the scientific sense. In "Signs of
the Times," an earlier essay which "Characteristics" to a
large extent complements, Carlyle described this manner of

thinking as mechanical and sadly acknowledged that "Mechanism" had become the "prevailing disposition of our spiritual nature itself." "Its implement," he elaborated, "is not Meditation, but Argument. 'Cause and effect' is almost the only category under which we look at, and work with, all Nature. Our first question with regard to any object is not, What is it? but, How is it? We are no longer instinctively driven to apprehend, and lay to heart, what is Good and Lovely, but rather to inquire, as onlookers, how it is produced, whence it comes, whither it goes" (CW 27:74). He mentioned in this context Adam Smith, David Hume, and Benjamin Constant. The list from which these names were drawn is potentially a long one, since Carlyle was talking about a longstanding tendency in British philosophy, beginning with Francis Bacon. And, rightly or wrongly, Carlyle always associated this British empirical strain with French rationalism, which accounts for the slightly anomalous presence of Constant in company with Smith and Hume. In "Characteristics," Constant's spot in the trio is more appropriately filled by Diderot, and the entire Anglo-French skeptical alliance is arrayed against Carlyle's various Germans, setting the stage, as it were, for a sort of philosophical Great War (cf. CW 28:40-41).

The thrust of Carlyle's reaction to modern skepticism, however, is not primarily philosophical. He displayed phenomenal enthusiasm and industry in his efforts to fathom the most formidable German philosophers, but, like the Editor in *Sartor Resartus,* his zeal was inevitably tempered by the intractability of the material and probably by his awareness of his own limitations. Philosophy was never more than one element, albeit an important element, in his quest to redefine and preserve the religious spirit in skeptical times. This was equally true of Emerson, whose native capacity for strict philosophical reasoning was surely no greater than Carlyle's. These men were writers, not philosophers. During the Transcendental period in their lives, roughly from the late 1820s to the late 1830s, both men wrote extensively on philosophical and theological topics. Yet what they produced was neither philosophy nor theology, but literature, a literature that, as Lawrence Buell intelligently comments on a passage in Emerson's Divinity School Address, dwelt "somewhere between metaphor and metaphysics, between the word as message and the word as art."[5]

Critics of the literature of ideas always find it necessary to abstract the ideas from the literature, even though the results are often reductive and distorted. Yet the effort is justifiable when responsibly applied to books like *Sartor Resartus* and Emerson's *Nature*, where a sure grip on the main ideas is an essential precondition to a true comprehension of the entire work when the ideas are returned to their literary context. If only for convenience, almost all these abstractions may be grouped under the heading "Transcendentalism." Though neither Carlyle nor Emerson embraced the term wholeheartedly, both used it frequently. Curiously, they both avoided too close an identification of the word with their own names. Carlyle usually applied it only to German philosophers, including, to be sure, his own Professor Teufelsdröckh. After *Sartor* he rarely used it at all. In 1835 Emerson and his friends considered founding a journal to be called *The Transcendentalist* or *The Spiritual Inquirer,* possibly with a transplanted Carlyle as editor, but the journal that finally emerged five years later was named *The Dial.* And when the Emerson circle began to hold formal meetings in 1836, the group was labeled the Transcendental Club by outsiders; the participants had other preferences.[6] Similarly, in his retrospective lecture "The Transcendentalist" (1841), Emerson never applied the word directly to himself, to Carlyle, or to any of their writings. The popularity of the term among his detractors may partly explain Emerson's ambivalence toward it, and Carlyle soon acquired a distaste for "isms" of any sort. Nonetheless, the word was associated with their names at the time and has remained so ever since, with or without their blessing.

The Transcendentalism of Carlyle and Emerson was, at bottom, a spiritual protest against the prevailing attitudes of rationalism, materialism, and skepticism which Carlyle condemned in "Signs of the Times" and "Characteristics." The religious aspects of Transcendentalism were sometimes more pronounced among Emerson and his followers than with Carlyle, partly because in America the mechanical mode of thought had attained formal expression in religion through the triumph of Unitarianism in New England. Everyone realized that Emerson's Divinity School Address (1838) was, literally, a direct assault on the Unitarian stronghold, Harvard's Divinity Hall, where it was delivered, and the American Unitarians immediately became the Emersonians' most bitter opponents. For Carlyle, the embodiment of the mechanical philosophy in Britain was Utilitarianism, which, of course, is not a religion. But the spiritual emptiness Carlyle perceived in the rationalism of the Utilitarians was very similar to the spiritual deadness Emerson challenged in his antagonists among the Unitarians. They both proclaimed rationalism, whether disguised as a social philosophy or as a theology, the enemy of the spirit and Transcendentalism the champion of the spirit.

In both Britain and America the conflict between Transcendentalism and rationalism was more than mere strife among parties. To preserve religion against the threat of rationalism, it was not enough to counterattack the rationalists. The essence of religion had to be defined, or redefined, before it could be revived. The Transcendentalists were widely condemned as enemies of religion because they were ruthless in their determination to strip away all that was superfluous or ossified in the old beliefs. Their purpose, however, was not to destroy religion, but, quite the opposite, to find the place where the spirit must live if the spirit can be said to exist at all. Unlike the Unitarians, who tried to establish a mode of faith acceptable to rationalism, the Transcendentalists sought first to define the minimal grounds of spiritual life, and then to defend that territory not only against the onslaught of skepticism, but even against the advance of reason.

It shoud be stressed that Transcendentalism, despite its religious spirit, was not a theological system, nor was it ever intended to develop into one. Representing Transcendentalism as a theological system would resemble Teufelsdröckh's error in regarding English dandies and Irish paupers as religious sects. But, to repeat, certain ideas concerning religion and the life of the spirit can be abstracted from the speculative writings of Carlyle and Emerson, especially from *Sartor Resartus* and *Nature*. Other pieces of theirs, along with the works of many other writers (from Coleridge to Theodore Parker), are also relevant, but, for our purposes at least, these two books may be thought of as the primary documents of Anglo-American Transcendentalism. At least they have a greater claim to consideration as religious statements than the "Fashionable Novels" which Teufelsdröckh took for the sacred texts of the Brummellites. Even so, in the following discussion of the religious basis of Transcendentalism, conducted (with a rather dry, but, I fear, unavoidable formality) under six subheadings, the obvious lesson of Teufelsdröckh's folly should be borne in mind by both writer and reader alike.

Idealism. A key chapter of *Nature* is entitled "Idealism," but the word is conspicuously absent in *Sartor Resartus*. However, Carlyle had already demonstrated his awareness of the close connection between idealism and Transcendentalism elsewhere. In a lengthy digression on "Kantism, or German metaphysics generally" included in an essay on "Novalis" (1829), he described an idealist as one who "boasts that his Philosophy is Transcendental, that is, 'ascending *beyond* the senses'; which, he asserts, *all* Philosophy, properly so called, by its nature is and must be . . . To a Transcendentalist, Matter has an existence, but only as a Phenomenon: were *we* not there, neither would it be there" (CW 27:24-25). Similarly, early in *Sartor Resartus* the Editor speaks of Teufelsdröckh's "Transcendental Philosophies, and humour of looking at all Matter and Material things as Spirit" (SR, p. 29), and in this manner the concept of idealism permeates the book even though the word itself never appears at all.

In "The Transcendentalist" Emerson was quite explicit about the centrality of idealism in his thought, declaring that what was "properly called Transcendentalism among us" was actually idealism (NAL, p. 201). With typical Emersonian dualism he immediately went on to divide all thinkers into "two sects, Materialists and Idealists," and in the present context this familiar distinction takes on added significance. For in order to establish the indispensable core of religious belief, it was necessary for Transcendentalism to denounce crude materialism at the very start. A conception of reality which adamantly refuses to admit the possible existence of anything which is not accessible to the senses must exclude all potential for religion. "The truth is," Carlyle observed in "Signs of the Times," "men have lost their belief in the Invisible, and believe only in the Visible; or, to speak it in other words: This is not a Religious age. Only the material, the immediately practical, not the divine and spiritual, is important to us" (CW 27:74).

The refutation of crude materialism and the consequent establishment of at least a minimal idealism are actually rather modest aims, for only the most naive materialist would maintain that all that is real must literally be "visible." Yet neither Carlyle nor Emerson was willing to accept the full implications of extreme idealism, which would deny the absolute existence of an external reality independent of thought. Even on theological grounds, Emerson wrote in Nature, this theory "does not satisfy the demands of the spirit" because it "leaves me in the splendid labyrinth of my perceptions, to wander without end" (NAL, pp. 37-38). But on the whole, Emerson was content to leave the question open; he would let extreme idealism stand as a "useful introductory hypothesis" (p. 38). For the *possibility* of an ideal universe is actually more important than its validity, which can never be determined anyway. "In my utter impotence to test the authenticity of the report of my senses, to know whether the impressions they make on me correspond with outlying objects," he asked in the "Idealism" chapter, "what difference does it make, whether Orion is up there in heaven, or some god paints the image in the firmament of the soul?" (p. 29).

In his article on "Novalis," Carlyle's position was just as problematic when he insisted that the materialist's faith in his senses had no more authority than the idealist's trust in the spirit (CW 27:24). But in *Sartor Resartus* Carlyle (or at least Carlyle as Teufelsdröckh) seemed to come much closer to endorsing idealism in its most extreme form. At one point Teufelsdröckh wonders whether "this solid-seeming World, after all, were but an air-image, our ME the only reality: and Nature . . . but the reflex of our own inward force" (*SR,* p. 55). Elsewhere he asserts that "Matter, were it never so despicable, is Spirit, the manifestation of Spirit: were it never so honourable, can it be more?" (pp. 66-67). But in declaring matter the "manifestation of Spirit," Teufelsdröckh proposes not the unreality but the *symbolic* nature of matter. "The thing Visible," the last *Sartor* passage continues, shifting into the language of the Clothes Philosophy, is "a Garment, a Clothing of the higher, celestial Invisible." Teufelsdröckh never denies material reality, but he does claim the existence of a higher, spiritual reality which material reality both reveals and conceals, in the manner of a garment draping an invisible form. (Emerson also describes nature as the symbol of spirit and speaks of "a necessity in spirit to manifest itself in material forms.") Carlyle's attitude probably remained consistent with an entry in his notebook from 1830. "I think I have got rid of Materialism," the passage tentatively begins, and it rather tentatively continues: "Matter no longer seems to me so ancient, so unsubduable, so *certain* and palpable as Mind. *I* am Mind; whether matter or not I know not — and care not."[7]

Carlyle generally asked no more from idealism than did Emerson. Like Teufelsdröckh, Emerson's Orphic poet also flirts with extreme idealism in the concluding paragraph of *Nature*. In effect, Teufelsdröckh and the Orphic poet are only pleading for the possible reality of the invisible when they hyperbolically assert the unreality of the visible. Their Transcendentalism is more than a modest idealism writ large, but it does rest, however shakily, on an idealistic foundation.

Logic and Intuition. Crude rationalism presented a challenge to the religious spirit similar to that of crude materialism. Where one refused to look beyond the senses, the other refused to think beyond the set patterns of logic. Logic in this sense corresponds to the "mechanical thinking" decried in "Signs of the Times." The response of Transcendentalism was complicated by the undeniable utility of logical thought even in its most mechanical form. Crude rationalism could not be dismissed out of hand like crude materialism. If religious beliefs are not accessible to ordinary logic, then another mode of thought must arise to supplement logic, though not to replace it altogether, for the utter denial of all logic leads to a position even more perilous than extreme idealism. A dualist epistemology necessarily results, since the continued validity of logic must be acknowledged after an additional, "higher" faculty has been established to redeem the truths which logic refutes.

Thus in "Signs of the Times" Carlyle balanced "mechanics" with "dynamics," which he defined as "a science which treats of . . . the primary, unmodified forces and energies of man, the mysterious springs of Love, and Fear, and Wonder, of Enthusiasm, Poetry, Religion, all which have a truly vital and *infinite* character" (CW 27:68). In "Characteristics" he used the terms adopted here, "logic" and "intuition," when he wrote that the "healthy Understanding . . . is not the Logical, argumentative, but the Intuitive; for the end of Understanding is not to prove and find reasons, but

to know and believe" (CW 28:5). He borrowed another pair
of terms, "reason" and "understanding," from Kant, but he
employed these terms in precisely the same manner as the
others. In the "Kantism" interlude in "Novalis," he spoke of
"the recognition, by these Transcendentalists, of a higher
faculty in man than Understanding; of Reason (*Vernunft*),
the pure, ultimate light of our nature" (CW 27:27).

"Kantian" and "non-Kantian" terms freely intermingle in
Sartor Resartus. One Kantian chapter is appropriately
named "Pure Reason"; yet in another, more important
chapter, "Symbols," the understanding, "our Logical, Men-
surative faculty," is surpassed not by the reason but by fantasy: "the organ of the Godlike" by means of which "Man
. . . though based, to all seeming, on the small Visible, does
nevertheless extend down into the infinite deeps of the Invisible" (*SR*, pp. 217-218). Logic, or the understanding,
easily becomes associated with materialism, just as intuition,
or the reason, is linked with idealism and consequently with
religion in general.

The same association occurs in the "Idealism" chapter of
Nature. "To the senses and the unrenewed understanding,
belongs a sort of instinctive belief in the absolute existence
of nature . . . Things are ultimates, and they never look beyond their sphere." This "despotism of the senses" is weakened by the intervention of the reason, through which "out-
lines and surfaces become transparent, and are no longer
seen; causes and spirits are seen through them," ultimately
leading to "the reverential withdrawing of nature before its
God" (*NAL*, p. 30). Although his knowledge of the Germans was entirely indirect, Emerson displayed greater bold-
ness than Carlyle in his use of Kant's terms. In the Divinity
School Address, for example, he referred to Christ's gospel
as a "doctrine of the Reason" (p. 81).

The distinction between logical and intuitive modes of
thought leads to pure mysticism if logic is dismissed completely. Neither man was prepared to go so far; as with
idealism, their aims were moderate and limited. All they

asked was the concession that the totality of the knowable may exceed the bounds of the rational. In other words, they were pleading the case for the invisible in the realm of thought as well as in the realm of matter.

Language. An ambivalence toward language echoes the Transcendental dualism regarding thought. On the one hand, language in the service of materialism and mechanism is fatal to the spirit. "What are your Axioms, and Categories, and Systems, and Aphorisms?" asks Teufelsdröckh. "Words," he answers, echoing Hamlet, "words. High Aircastles are cunningly built of Words, the Words well bedded also in good Logic-mortar; wherein, however, no Knowledge will come to lodge" (*SR*, p. 54). Emerson's indictment of the "corruption of language," when "duplicity and falsehood take place of simplicity and truth" (*NAL*, p. 20), reflects a similar distrust.

But language can also serve the intuition. Both *Sartor Resartus* and *Nature* stress the origin of language in "metaphors": Teufelsdröckh feels that all language is metaphorical (p. 73), and Emerson claims language was originally "all poetry" (p. 19). Because metaphors and poetry are fashioned and comprehended intuitively, often at the expense of common logic, writers of poetry are able to express intuited truths that are inaccessible to logic.

Emerson speculated that the metaphorical nature of language may correspond to the spiritual essence of reality. He suggested this most economically in *Nature* at the beginning of the chapter on "Language," where the outline form he employed bears a peculiar resemblance to, of all things, the syllogism of formal logic:

1. Words are signs of natural facts.

2. Particular natural facts are symbols of particular spiritual facts.

3. Nature is the symbol of spirit. (*NAL*, p. 17)

Here the language of logic itself becomes the language of poetry.

Infinity: Space and Time. Carlyle derived from Kant his concept of the ideality of space and time, which in one respect might be regarded merely as another way of establishing the ideality of matter. The concept serves just this purpose in "Novalis," where, once the "absolute existence" of space and time is denied, "Matter is itself annihilated; and the black Spectre, Atheism . . . melts into nothingness forever" (CW 27:26). Carlyle also used this idea in his approach to the subject of miracles, for if the laws of space and time are ultimately meaningless, then occurrences in violation of those laws are no less remarkable than everyday events in compliance with them. (More will be said about miracles later.)

The most interesting and perhaps the most important use of the words "space" and "time" concerns the Transcendental preoccupation with the infinite. Unlike most ideas traditionally associated with metaphysical speculation, the concept of infinity received support rather than derision from science, especially from astronomy. The scientific model of the universe, to put it briefly, had undergone a literally boundless expansion, both in extent and duration. Carlyle hoped to endow the now infinite universe with a spiritual dimension. For this purpose his familiarity with astronomy (he once hoped for a professorship) was as helpful as his acquaintance with Kant. In the concluding paragraph of "Signs of the Times," he wrote of the endlessness rather than the nonexistence of space and time, but the spiritual message, so far as he was concerned, was the same. Just as the Earth, he said, "is journeying with its fellows through infinite Space, so are the wondrous destinies embarked on it journeying through infinite Time, under a higher guidance than ours . . . Go where it will, the deep HEAVEN will be around it. Therein let us have hope and sure faith" (CW 27:82). A comparable paragraph ends "Characteristics," along with a further suggestion, characteristically phrased as a rhetorical question: "Do we not already know that the name of the Infinite is GOOD, is GOD?" (CW 28:43).

Carlyle apparently believed that insofar as science affirmed an infinite universe, it was possible to demonstrate a scientific basis for an almost supernatural concept. This "spiritual" approach to infinity, along with the idealistic view of space and time Carlyle extracted from Kant, should be borne in mind when reading *Sartor Resartus*. Teufelsdröckh's capacity for alluding to infinity and eternity is itself nearly infinite. He defines a man, when observed by "the eye of Pure Reason," as one who "sees and fashions for himself a Universe, with azure Starry spaces, and long Thousands of Years." The phrase "fashions for himself" underscores the *ideality* of the infinite; it is infinite because the reason so perceives it. But in this case, for once, empirical observation — the understanding, if you will — corroborates the intuited truth.

Infinity is a natural ally of the spirit because it stimulates a sense of wonder. Teufelsdröckh speaks lovingly of the "high worth of universal Wonder" (*SR,* p. 67), and wonder in the infinite abounds in Emerson's speculative writings as well. The bizarre "transparent eyeball" passage in *Nature,* to take a well known example, begins with Emerson standing in the woods, his "head bathed by the blithe air, and uplifted into infinite space" (*NAL,* p. 10). Only when seen from an infinite perspective does the universe become unified. Emerson could also treat space and time in a more explicitly "Kantian" sense (cf. pp. 24-25). Like Carlyle, he appreciated the mystery of the infinite, a mystery which rational philosophies could not explain away and yet could not deny.

Miracles. The Transcendentalists' position on miracles rapidly became the *bête noire* of the New England Unitarians, especially after Emerson delivered his Divinity School Address in July 1838. The oration condemns "the very word

Miracle, as pronounced by Christian churches . . .; it is
Monster" (*NAL*, p. 81). A month later Emerson was denounced by the so-called "Unitarian Pope," Andrews Norton, in a newspaper; Carlyle, "that hyper-Germanized Englishman," Norton dismissed as a fairly harmless buffoon
who "as an original, might be tolerated, if one could forget
his imitators and admirers."[8] In October Emerson, who had
been begging Carlyle to come to America, felt the situation
was serious enough to warn his friend to stay home (L, pp.
196-197). For his part, Carlyle rejoiced over the "tempest in
a washbowl," delighted, perhaps, that Emerson's rupture
with organized religion was now irreversible. After praising
another Emerson oration he impatiently asked, "Where is
the heterodox Divinity one; which . . . b[rings] Goethe,
Transcendentalism and Carlyle into question, and on the
whole evinces 'what dif[ference] New England also makes
between *Pan*theism and *Pot*-theism'? I long to see that; I
expect to congratulate you on that too" (p. 200). Unfortunately the pamphlet kept getting lost in the mail, and Carlyle did not read it until 1839 (p. 214). By then the tempest
had died down, along with Carlyle's interest.

Emerson's qualified denial of the biblical miracles, which
provoked the controversy, is actually a minor aspect of the
Transcendental approach to the subject, and the main premise, the miraculousness of the mundane, was hardly a
revolutionary idea even then. As a Unitarian minister, the
young Emerson himself defended the New Testament miracles in one sermon and in another told his congregation,
"Go out into a garden and examine a seed; examine the
same plant in the bud and in the fruit, and you must confess
the whole process a miracle, a perpetual miracle."[9] By the
time he wrote *Nature,* Emerson may have decided that a
sufficient elaboration of the latter conception of miracles
obviated the need for an explicit refutation of the former.
"The invariable mark of wisdom is to see the miraculous in
the common," he wrote near the end of *Nature* (p. 44), and
he went on to speak of the "gaudy fable" people invent "to

hide the baldness of the fact." In other words, everyday life is wonderful in itself even without the occasional intervention of supernatural forces: "A fact is true poetry, and the most beautiful of fables. These wonders are brought to our own door." The implied obverse of all this, that a belief in "gaudy fables" is the invariable mark of ignorance, did not become dangerously clear until the Divinity School Address. There, predictably, it is not ignorance but "the understanding" which declares Christ "Jehovah come down out of heaven" and adds for good measure "I will kill you, if you say he was a man" (*NAL*, p. 81). (Christ himself, it will be remembered, preached a "doctrine of the Reason.") To an Andrews Norton, needless to say, the Kantian distinction amounted to no more than a subterfuge for irreverence.

Carlyle held the same attitude toward miracles, although he generally preferred to disregard rather than deny traditional views. In his essay on "Voltaire" (1829), his ideas and terminology anticipated Emerson's iconoclasm at Divinity College, but his tone was so moderate and conciliatory that had the essay appeared a decade later, it might even have slipped past Norton. To put it briefly, he tacitly conceded to Voltaire the terms of his skepticism, all the while deploring Voltaire's intentions in expressing them (cf. CW 26: 457-458). He was content to affirm the miraculous in the common and let others draw the inferences regarding the common sense of the miraculous. In his private notebook he applied this strategy to his own thinking and, humorously, to his own person: "Miracle? What is a Miracle? Can there be a thing more miraculous than any other thing? I myself am a standing wonder."[10]

Like their wonder before the infinite, the celebration of everyday miracles by the Transcendentalists attained a certain legitimacy from Science, the supposed enemy of all mystery, and even from technology, the embodiment of mechanical thinking. Thus when Teufelsdröckh speaks of "the grand Thaumaturgic art of Thought," meaning the power of the human mind to perform miracles, one of his examples is the steam engine, "stronger than any other Enchanter's Familiar" (*SR*, p. 118). Emerson also speaks of steam in a similar sense (*NAL*, pp. 11-12). Knowing how something works should not detract from its awesomeness, any more than its apparent inexplicability should establish an event as a miracle. "Can there be a thing more miraculous than any other thing?"

Morality. Morality, traditionally a province of religion, persists even in the most thoroughgoing skepticism, short of utter nihilism. The most salient differences between rational and religious moral systems usually reside not so much in which ethical precepts are proposed as in how they are to be enforced. The fine phrases notwithstanding, rational codes of morality, such as the Utilitarian principle of "the greatest happiness for the greatest number," are mainly governed by external rather than internal monitors, or, as Carlyle explained in "Signs of the Times," "not by greater love of Virtue, but by greater perfection of Police; and of that far subtler and stronger Police, called Public Opinion" (CW 27:78). The greater efficacy of an internally sanctioned morality was obvious to Carlyle and Emerson and constituted for them another powerful claim for the life of the spirit. "Foolish Wordmonger and Motive-grinder," Teufelsdröckh chides the Benthamite, "who in thy Logic-mill hast an earthly mechanism for the Godlike itself, and wouldst fain grind me out Virtue from the husks of Pleasure, —I tell thee, Nay!" The "terrors of Conscience," he elaborates, cannot be replaced by "diseases of the Liver." Morality is not a practical matter like cookery, and a censer is not a frying pan (*SR*, pp. 160-161). Any morality worthy of the name must have some spiritual element, just as any religion worthy of the name must have an ethical spirit. Caught in the clutches of the Everlasting No, Teufelsdröckh is saved from suicide by "a certain aftershine (*Nachschein*) of Christianity"; the content of this "aftershine," revealed a few pages earlier, is for the most part morality, "the Infinite nature of Duty still dimly present to me" (*SR,* pp. 165, 162). In his Divinity School Address, Emerson also affirmed the indestructability of the "moral sentiment," which "lies at the foundation of society, and successively creates all forms of worship" (*NAL,* p. 79).

The final step in the triumph of morality, its extension to the entire physical universe, represents the culmination of the Transcendental quest to isolate and preserve the essence of religion. "All things are moral," Emerson wrote in *Nature,* "and in their boundless changes have an unceasing reference to spiritual nature." Perceived intuitively, or according to the reason, all natural processes "hint or thunder to man the laws of right and wrong, and echo the Ten Commandments" (*NAL,* pp. 25-26). And for Teufelsdröckh, a moral universe is a living universe, a universe "not dead and demoniacal, a charnel-house with spectres"—like the Utilitarian universe—"but godlike, and my Father's!" (*SR,* p. 188). If idealism is the foundation of Transcendentalism, morality is the crown. A spiritual universe must be a moral universe.

In 1849 Carlyle was asked "if Emerson's ideas could be regarded as original." He replied, the inquirer reports, "that Emerson had, in the first instance, taken his system out of 'Sartor' and other of his (Carlyle's) writings, but he worked it out in a way of his own."[11] The significance of this statement lies not in its accuracy nor in its modesty, for it has little of either. Both Emerson and Carlyle took their ideas from a wide variety of sources, and whatever concepts and terms Emerson received through Carlyle actually originated elsewhere. Of greater interest is the apparent recognition by Carlyle that his speculative writings and those of Emerson can in fact be reduced to roughly the same abstract system, such as that constructed in the foregoing pages. This does not, however, mean that the essence of the religious thought of both writers is identical or that the differences between them are purely formal or stylistic. The similarities, it is true, outnumber the differences, but the differences are far more subtle and perhaps more profound. To find the differences, the abstractions must be returned to their living contexts. To see how each writer "worked it out in a way of his own," the integrity of the literature they created must be restored.

There are, of course, obvious differences of literary form and style. Emerson's instrument is the essay or lecture, where author addresses reader without intermediary. *Sartor Resartus* is written as a novel with two narrator/protagonists, Teufelsdröckh and the Editor, and these characters bear a complex relation to the author, Carlyle. In his indispensable study, *Sartor Called Resartus,* G. B. Tennyson neatly describes a typical strategy Carlyle employs throughout the book:

> Teufelsdröckh can urge the most radical measures, to the extreme annoyance of the Editor. But all the while Carlyle is building the conviction in the reader that what Teufelsdröckh says is truly consequential and deserves our hearing. The Editor habitually warns the reader against Teufelsdröckh, cautioning him not to be taken in by radical notions, or he throws up his hands in despair over Teufelsdröckh's incomprehensibility. At the same time, the Editor excerpts in such a way that Teufelsdröckh's ideas are given prominence, and the Editor himself is at last won over.[12]

One effect of this method is that, for the most part, Teufelsdröckh's words cannot be placed in Carlyle's mouth unless the moderating tones of the Editor are also taken into account. The Editor's role, "to build a firm Bridge for British travellers" through the Teutonic chaos to Teufelsdröckh's message (*SR,* p. 79), is, of course, the same role Carlyle played with regard to real German philosophers in his review articles. For most of *Sartor Resartus,* therefore, it is necessary to split Carlyle in two, since he is both Transcendental philosopher and skeptical "translator" and interpreter.

But in a deeper sense, Carlyle does at times speak through Teufelsdröckh directly. It is well known that many of the details of Teufelsdröckh's biography parallel events in Carlyle's own life; in particular, Carlyle claimed that the climax of the plot of *Sartor Resartus,* Teufelsdröckh's victory over the Everlasting No, occurred "quite literally" to Carlyle himself a decade earlier (*SR,* pp. 166-169 and n.). It is certainly important, though in itself such an identification of author with hero is not remarkable. Disguised autobiography, after all, is a standard technique in fiction. Carlyle still remains divided between Teufelsdröckh and Editor. But *Sartor Resartus* reverses a key aspect of the relationship between British reviewer and German philosopher that he had established in his earlier essays, and the effect of this reversal is to unify at crucial moments the voices of Carlyle and Teufelsdröckh. To appreciate the reversal, it is first necessary to examine his procedure in an earlier essay, for instance in the "Kantian" segment of "Novalis."

In that essay Carlyle ascribes to Kant the ideality of space and time, and, in a passage cited previously, he extends the concept to form a refutation of "that black Spectre, Atheism." Now it is only the specific philosophical idea of the "accidental character" of space and time that he actually attributes to Kant. The theological extension of the idea is attributed to no one in particular, or it would be more correct to say that Carlyle implicitly takes responsibility for it himself. This is accomplished with considerable subtlety. He begins with a brief paragraph on Kant's conception of time and space as "carefully deduced in his *Critik der reinen Vernunft*" (CW 27:25-26). At this point he makes no reference to religion, for he had found none in Kant.

The next paragraph begins with Carlyle's defense of the seriousness of German Transcendentalism in general. As an example, he chooses the time and space idea; "We shall find," he writes, "that to the Kantist it yields, almost immediately, a remarkable result of this sort." Instead of naming Kant, it will be observed, Carlyle has shifted to more general terms, such as "the Kantist." He also uses the neutral first person plural. "If Time and Space have no absolute existence, no existence out of our minds, it removes a stumbling-block from the very threshold of our Theology." The stumbling block gone, Carlyle rapidly steps up the pace. "For on this ground, when we say that the Deity is omnipresent and eternal . . . , we say nothing wonderful: nothing but that He also created Time and Space, that Time and Space are not laws of His being, but only of ours. Nay to the Transcendentalist," and so on to the annihilation of matter and the destruction of atheism (p. 26). He does not again name Kant until the end of the paragraph, when he returns to the limited proposition he had found in the *Critique of Pure Reason,* "that the logical method of the mind is arbitrary, so to speak, and might have been different." He follows a similar procedure when he discusses the understanding and the reason, another element in his philosophy borrowed from Kant, in "State of German Literature." "Will the Kantists forgive us," he asks self-defensively, "for the loose and popular manner in which we must here speak of these things, to bring them in any measure before the eyes of our readers?" (CW 26:83).

The difference between this pattern and what happens in *Sartor* should be clear. In the essays, the German philosopher proposes a restricted idea which in itself has no apparent theological significance. In explaining and elaborating the proposition, Carlyle himself draws the religious inferences. In *Sartor Resartus* Teufelsdröckh performs both these functions, providing both the concept and the theological extension of the concept. The Editor's role is not to elaborate but to modify or even to undercut Teufelsdröckh's pronouncements, though eventually, as G. B. Tennyson explains, he is himself converted and practically becomes Teufelsdröckh's disciple.

This discipleship is most pronounced in the chapter that the Editor speaks of as the "stupendous Section, headed *Natural Supernaturalism.*" After two paragraphs of ecstatic

introduction, the Editor reverently disappears. It is argu-
able that Teufelsdröckh disappears as well, along with his
Clothes Philosophy, which, the Editor explains, has been
subdued and now "attains to Transcendentalism" (*SR*, p.
255). The only extended clothes metaphor in the chapter is
the fable of Fortunatus' hat, which serves merely as an illustrative device in the section on space and time. Perhaps one
other clothes metaphor is pertinent: Carlyle has removed his
own clothes, the entire fiction of Editor, Teufelsdröckh, and
Clothes Philosophy. His purpose in this chapter is too important to admit any form of indirection. "In a word," the
Editor writes, "he has looked fixedly on Existence, till, one
after the other, its earthly hulls and garnitures have all
melted away; and now, to his rapt vision, the interior celestial Holy of Holies lies disclosed" (p. 255). Here will be
found the highest reach of Carlyle's grasp for God. Before,
he never spoke so openly; after, he will never speak publicly
again. After *Sartor Resartus* his published statements on
religion are confined to brief, scattered, and usually digres-
sive remarks in quite other contexts. "Pantheism, Potthe-
ism, Mydoxy, Thydoxy are nothing at all to me," reads a
typical comment, from the letter to Emerson about the
Divinity School controversy: "a weariness the whole jargon,
which I avoid speaking of, decline listening to" (L, p. 200).
"Natural Supernaturalism" is the culmination not only of
Sartor Resartus, but of Carlyle's career as a speculative
writer and perhaps of his whole spiritual life as well.

To a greater or lesser degree, all the elements of the
Transcendental project to determine and preserve the essence of religion are in "Natural Supernaturalism," but the
chapter is more than just another exploration of the theological possibilities of miracles in everyday events and the
ideality of space and time. Carlyle does repeat many of these
arguments in his most emphatic manner, heightening his
language through such means as extensive reliance on the
present tense and the accumulation of potent nondeclara-
tive sentences. Such techniques are common throughout

Sartor Resartus, but here their use is greatly intensified. G. B. Tennyson, for example, finds "by actual count, almost three-fourths as many interrogative sentences as declarative ones," and he quotes a passage in which five out of six sentences are exclamations. The purpose of this stylistic intensification, Tennyson believes, is "to involve the reader," "to engage the reader in the act of comprehending and pursuing the clothes philosophy," and second to illustrate "the annihilation of time itself."[13] This is all very true, but it does not go far enough, at least not with regard to "Natural Supernaturalism." What is Carlyle questioning in these forty-five interrogative sentences? Elsewhere, in a different context, Tennyson observes that the chapter is "cast in the form of an imaginary dialogue, or even argument . . . Teufelsdröckh himself poses the questions, attributing them to disbelievers; then he provides the answers."[14] But who are these "disbelievers"? They are identified once as "several" and once as "an illuminated class" (p. 256); everywhere else, Carlyle uses the second person: "thou" or "you." All through *Sartor Resartus* the second person is often employed, in Tennyson's words, "for Teufelsdröckh's dialogue with himself and in direct address to the reader."[15] Surely this chapter is no exception. Admittedly, the initial sarcasms directed at the "illuminated class" recall his frequent polemics against the "Motive-grinders" and other enemies of the spirit, but in "Natural Supernaturalism" this tone quickly fades as the questions themselves lose their philistinism and become serious religious inquiries in their own right. The "illuminated class" asks, " 'But is it not the deepest Law of Nature that she be constant?' " (p. 256). It is a very different sort of inquirer who a few pages later asks, "And seest thou therein any glimpse of IMMORTALITY?" (p. 262). The "illuminated class" has vanished along with the internal quotation marks. Carlyle, or Teufelsdröckh, is no longer merely posing rhetorical questions at all; he is asking real questions. And another function of the intensified use of the present tense in this chapter is to underscore the fact that Carlyle himself is really looking for answers.

In "Natural Supernaturalism" he presents in the best possible light the Transcendental redefinition of religious belief and, in effect, asks: does it work? Is it, after all, a sufficient answer to the challenge of skepticism? And does it constitute a sure foundation for a return to faith? The natural and the supernatural have been alienated from each other by rationalism and materialism, by science and by "custom"; can they ever be reunited? Carlyle hopes they can, but he must ask some hard questions before he can be certain. "What is Philosophy throughout but a continual battle against Custom; an ever-renewed effort to *transcend* the sphere of blind Custom, and so become Transcendental?" (p. 259).

The questions proliferate, one merging into another. First comes "the question of questions": "What specially is a Miracle?" (p. 255). Carlyle supplies the expected answer. An event seems miraculous only to an observer who does not understand *how* it occurs, but every event is miraculous to those who realize that no one will ever fully understand *why* it occurs. But now he makes evident his awareness of the inevitable objection, that a miraculous account of the common demands the irreverence of a common sense explanation for the miraculous, from which it follows that a "supernatural" belief in the miraculous is a symptom of ignorance or lunacy. He comes dangerously close to that admission (which is hardly different from the skepticism of, say, Voltaire) when he offers his agreement at one point with contemporary psychology that "Witchcraft and all manner of Spectre-work and Demonology" are evidence of "Madness and Diseases of the Nerves." This apparent digression comes at the very end of the first discussion of miracles; a small gap in the text follows the end of the paragraph (pp. 259-260). The cause-and-effect relation of insanity to a belief in miracles is the unavoidable inference. At best it is a question of language, of the "potency of Names." "What is Madness,"

he asks, "what are Nerves?" "Was Luther's Picture of the
Devil less a Reality, whether it was formed within the bodily
eye, or without it?" And what of Luther's, or Carlyle's, picture of God?

The remainder of the chapter (pp. 260-267) ostensibly
concerns, again, the relative existence of space and time,
but it is really a questioning of the prospects for immortality. Carlyle had admitted his fear of death in "The Everlasting No," and his defiance of it is the most salient fact in
Teufelsdröckh's "conversion" experience on the "Rue Saint-
Thomas de l'Enfer": "I asked myself: 'What *art* thou afraid
of? . . . what is the sum-total of the worst that lies before
thee? Death? Well, Death; and say the pangs of Tophet too
. . . Let it come, then; I will meet it and defy it!' And as I so
thought, there rushed like a stream of fire over my soul; and
I shook base Fear away from me forever" (p. 167). Defiance
of the fear of death, however, is not the same as victory over
death itself. "Blind Custom" would regard such a victory
over death as inseparable from religion in the most "supernatural" sense, involving faith in the afterlife. The closing
pages of "Natural Supernaturalism" represent a heroic
struggle for that victory in the arena of Transcendentalism.

Two paragraphs more on the ideality of space and time
("Fortunatus' hat") begin the discussion; the searching questions resume in the third. "Or thinkest thou it were impossible, unimaginable? Is the Past annihilated, then, or only
past; is the Future non-extant, or only future?" (p. 261).
Through the "mystic faculties" of memory and hope, past
and future exist in the present: "Yesterday and Tomorrow
both *are*," at least in the imagination. When he extends this
philosophical idea to embrace God's "universal HERE" and
"everlasting NOW" (p. 262), he has advanced as far as his
editorial elaboration of Kant in "Novalis," where he used
the same words (CW 27:26). But the attempt to go beyond,
to stretch these ideas far enough to attain a promise of immortality, fails; the system collapses in upon itself.

And seest thou therein any glimpse of IMMORTALITY? —
O Heaven! Is the white Tomb of our Loved One, who died from
our arms, and had to be left behind us there, which rises in the
distance, like a pale, mournfully receding Milestone, to tell
how many toilsome uncheered miles we have journeyed on
alone, — but a pale spectral Illusion! Is the lost Friend still mysteriously Here, even as we are Here mysteriously, with God! —
Know of a truth that only the Time-shadows have perished, or
are perishable; that the real Being of whatever was, and whatever is, and whatever will be, *is* even now and forever. (*SR*, p.
262)

To say that "we" — the dead and the living — are all "with
God" is indeed to see the miraculous in the common, to use
the language of intuition to refute the logical proposition
that all must die. The effort is heroic, but the result is un-
convincing, even for Carlyle himself. The implied admission
comes immediately, if reluctantly: "Believe it thou must;
understand it thou canst not." To encompass immortality,
Carlyle is forced to abandon Transcendentalism, or rather
to see through Transcendentalism and retreat to the supernatural, to faith, to the bankrupt old beliefs. An "intuited
truth" turns out to be nothing more than an asserted wish.

The sad and frightening coda arrives after a few more
pages on space, time, and miracles. We are all ghosts, he
explains, but our ghostliness is a reflection not of our prospects for eternal life, but of the very certainty and universality of our death. "Are we not Spirits, that are shaped into a
body, into an Appearance; and that fade away again into
air and Invisibility? This is no metaphor, it is a simple scientific *fact;* we start out of Nothingness, take figure, and are
Apparitions; round us, as round the veriest spectre, is Eternity" (p. 264). (Already he is thinking of his favorite Shake-
spearean passage, the lines from *The Tempest* — "We are
such stuff as dreams are made of," and so on — with which he
will close the chapter, lines that may suggest a kind of after-

life but might with equal justice assert the meaninglessness of life and the oblivion which precedes and follows life.)

The final, terrifying image in "Natural Supernaturalism" is a universal *danse macabre,* "our mad Dance of the Dead." Part of the inspiration for the use of this ancient motif probably comes from a graveyard vision of Richter's which Carlyle translated in 1830 (CW 27:155-158). Tennyson demonstrates in detail the close correlation between the Richter piece and "The Everlasting No."[16] As Richter awoke from his nightmare and joyfully prayed to God, so Teufelsdröckh in the earlier chapters of *Sartor Resartus* found salvation in "The Everlasting Yea." But no such affirmation is found here, for the dancing apparitions Carlyle envisions in the concluding paragraphs of "Natural Supernaturalism" are the living inhabitants of his own world, including himself, now alive but soon to die. "O Heaven, it is mysterious, it is awful to consider that we not only carry each a future Ghost within Him; but are, in very deed, Ghosts! These Limbs, whence had we them; this stormy Force; this life-blood with its burning Passion? They are dust and shadow" (p. 265). Carlyle sees his own death, and although he thinks he has overcome the fear of death, he now realizes that there is no hope of ever seeing beyond death. All that is visible is the spectacle of rampaging generations: "We emerge from the Inane; haste stormfully across the astonished Earth; then plunge again into the Inane" (p. 266).

The last words of the chapter recall the courage of Teufelsdröckh's triumph over fear, but they also reflect the resignation of a Transcendentalist whose philosophical limits fall short of his religious aspirations. "But whence? — O Heaven, whither?" These final questions are the most expressive and the most dangerous of all the questions in this chapter of questions. Carlyle probably should not have asked them; he should have heeded the caution of Teufelsdröckh, who, even at his zenith of affirmation in "The Everlasting Yea," asks "What words, known to these profane times, speak, even afar-off, of the unspeakable?" (p. 185).

Those two little biblical-sounding archaisms, *whence* and *whither,* question the unquestionable. Transcendentalism cannot answer; neither logic nor intuition can answer. There is no answer. "Sense knows not; Faith knows not; only that it is through Mystery to Mystery, from God and to God."

John Sterling, Carlyle's friend and probably the first serious reader of *Sartor Resartus,* recognized in these words the inevitable failure of Transcendentalism as a new gateway to religious belief. Sterling wrote to Carlyle that Teufelsdröckh simply "does not believe in a God"; furthermore, the state of Teufelsdröckh's feelings at the end of "Natural Supernaturalism"

> tallies with the whole strain of his character. What we find everywhere, with an abundant use of the name of God, is the conception of a formless Infinite whether in time or space; of a high inscrutable Necessity, which it is the chief wisdom and virtue to submit to, which is the mysterious impersonal base of all Existence, — shows itself in the laws of every separate being's nature; and for man in the shape of duty. On the other hand, I affirm, we do know whence we come and whither we go! —

Years later, Sterling referred to *Sartor* as "a litany of despair." In his reply to Sterling's letter, Carlyle expressed the same contempt for "Pantheist" and "Pottheist" that he would one day exhibit to Emerson. He commended Sterling's faith and denied the charge against Teufelsdröckh, but all in an ambiguous, really empty manner which Charles Frederick Harrold considers an early taste of "late-Victorian religious vagueness and rhetoric."[17] Had Carlyle ever again produced anything at all extensive on the subject of religious belief, he would probably have written in the banal mode of his letter to Sterling. It is to his credit that he preferred a rigid adherence to his "Gospel of Silence." "Speech is of Time," says Teufelsdröckh, "Silence is of Eternity." For his part, Sterling remained with the Church of England.

Carlyle actually did make one other attempt at religious speculation of a Transcendental nature. This is the curious fragment with the almost Emersonian title, "Spiritual Optics," which he wrote in 1852 and never published. According to Froude, who includes it in his biography, Carlyle "said that it contained his real conviction, a conviction that lay at the bottom of all his thought about man and man's doings in this world." The central idea, that the "miraculous" and "divine" are subjective or "the effect of optics," is really no more than a simplified and rather diluted restatement of the speculations of his youth. It is the Clothes Philosopher as optometrist. Modern readers, particularly physicists, may find striking his use of an observer in a railroad car as a metaphor for spiritual perception and his search at one point for a "*word* to express that extensive or universal operation of referring the motion from yourself to the object you look at, or *vice versa?* Is there none?"[18] (A pity he did not hit on "relativity"!) But if he was onto something new, he never developed it further. Toward the end of *Sartor Resartus* the Editor says of Teufelsdröckh that "in everthing he was still scenting-out Religion" (p. 287). "Spiritual Optics" shows that at least Carlyle remained always on the scent.

In the conversation I mentioned before about Emerson's originality, Carlyle also complained about Emerson's writings "suddenly stopping short and leading to nothing."[19] We have seen that on the one occasion when Carlyle himself refused to stop short, his path led nowhere and he was left dangling. Instead of the direct route, Emerson indeed preferred "stopping short" and starting again on a new tangent. He would never arrive at the goal, but the goal may not have existed in the first place. And unlike Carlyle, he could proceed on his journeys forever: he was able to continue speculating about religious belief almost until his death precisely because he refused to pursue, beyond the limits he himself set, the kinds of questions Carlyle grappled with in "Natural

Supernaturalism." Within the confines of Transcendentalism, Emerson paradoxically found infinite freedom.

He would not have described Carlyle's spiritual life in the sense in which it has been depicted here, at least not exactly. At the beginning of *English Traits,* it will be recalled, he spoke of Carlyle's "disinclination" to bruise himself against walls and "to place himself where no step can be taken." In the same way, his most direct comment on "Natural Supernaturalism," a journal entry from December 1835, criticized Carlyle for not going far enough and reiterated his dismissal of Carlyle's credentials as a philosopher. Carlyle, he wrote, "seems to me most limited in this chapter or speculation in which they regard him as most original & profound — I mean in his Religion & immortality from the removal of Time & Space. He seems merely to work with an alien foreign thought not to live in it himself."[20] Insofar as he must have realized that "Natural Supernaturalism" was Carlyle's most ambitious attempt at profundity, his reaction was astonishingly unsympathetic. But Emerson by this time had reached the treacherous point in his intellectual development where he was almost ready to try his hand at some "original speculation" of his own, but as yet he had produced nothing of substance. Thus the standard against which he measured Carlyle was the yet unwritten speculative work evolving in his own mind, and it is not surprising that Carlyle came off second best when Emerson set the actual against the potential. After undergoing the experience of composing *Nature,* he may have looked more charitably, and perhaps more perceptively, on Carlyle's "Religion & immortality from the removal of Time & Space." The journal remark is candid, but it should be considered an initial reaction rather than a mature judgment.

His attitude toward *Sartor Resartus* as a whole, at the time as well as in later years, was anything but straightforward. On the one hand, his genuine admiration for the book and its author needed no further demonstration than his labors in getting it published and promoted. But alongside this championship stands the recollection, many years later, of his friend James Elliot Cabot that

> Emerson was not among the enthusiasts for "Sartor" when it first appeared here; his preface, some of them thought, was timid and superfluously apologetic; and when I tried, long afterwards, to recall to him the stir the book made in the minds of some of the younger men, he hesitated, and said he supposed he had got all that earlier, from Coleridge. He was in full sympathy with the ideas, but the "masquerade" under which they were presented was so displeasing to him as to make him doubtful how it would be received if reprinted here.[21]

It is not possible to tell whether in the last sentence Cabot was recalling a conversation with Emerson or referring to Emerson's preface to the American edition of *Sartor*. In any case, Carlyle "enthusiasts" may well have used stronger language than "timid" and "superfluously apologetic" in describing the unsigned "Preface of the American Editors." Carlyle, in thanking Emerson for the American edition, mentioned the "Preface to it such as no kindest friend could have improved" (L, p. 154), and he reprinted it in the first English edition of 1838. Nevertheless, interlinear criticism and perhaps even a hint of accusation are faintly discernible in the preface, especially where Emerson writes of Carlyle's "humor to advance the gravest speculations upon the gravest topics in a quaint and burlesque style. If his masquerade offend any of his audience, to that degree that they will not hear what he has to say, it may chance to draw others to listen to his wisdom; and what work of imagination can hope to please all?"[22] The witty metaphor may have been intended only as an introductory adumbration of the Clothes Philosophy. But a "masquerade," of course, suggests clothing of a special kind, such as the disguise of a reveler at a ball.

The word "masquerade" also appears in the first paragraph of *Nature,* which was published just a few months after the American *Sartor*. Perhaps Emerson is paying homage to Carlyle by emulating his method when, in reference to the theology and philosophy inherited from previous centuries, he asks, "Why should we grope among the dry bones of the past, or put the living generation into masquerade out of its faded wardrobe?" (*NAL*, p. 7). Another parallel between the "Introduction" to *Nature* and *Sartor Resartus*, however, would be far more difficult to construe as commendatory. The Editor begins the first chapter of *Sartor* with a whimsical list of various triumphs of modern knowledge. Why, he asks, has science overlooked the most obvious subject, clothes, "which Man's Soul wears as its outermost wrappage and overall; wherein his whole other Tissues are included and screened, his whole Faculties work, his whole Self lives, moves, and has its being?" (p. 5). The last part of the question playfully alludes to the Bible: "For in him we live, and move, and have our being" (Acts 17.28). Compare the third paragraph of *Nature,* which expresses similar ideas. Here Emerson's tone is much more formal, even solemn, than it is in the book as a whole:

> All science has one aim, namely, to find a theory of nature. We have theories of races and of functions, but scarcely yet a remote approach to an idea of creation. We are now so far from the road to truth, that religious teachers dispute and hate each other, and speculative men are esteemed unsound and frivolous. But to a sound judgment, the most abstract truth is the most practical. Whenever a true theory appears, it will be its own evidence. Its test is, that it will explain all phenomena. (*NAL*, p. 8)

What this seems to add up to is Emerson's opinion that his book, no less than Carlyle's, offers "the gravest speculations on the gravest topics," but without the "quaint and burlesque style" and without the "masquerade." Speculative men, he felt, should not be "esteemed unsound and frivolous." I do not mean to imply that he thought Carlyle really was either; he probably meant that the enemies of Transcendentalism might accuse Carlyle of frivolity and unsound-ness of mind (as indeed they did, including Emerson, for all his caution, in the condemnation). He appreciated Carlyle's sense of humor but, as he told him in 1834, he questioned the propriety of lavishing "Celestial truths" on it.

Emerson succeeds in avoiding frivolity when he expounds the same celestial truths in *Nature,* and he is even more successful in avoiding the grim realities which wrecked Carlyle's Transcendental hopes in "Natural Supernaturalism." Not that he disregarded the questions that Carlyle pursued into the abyss: in the chapter of *Nature* called "Spirit" he confronts two of the most important: "Whence is matter? and Whereto?" But Emerson's answers to whence and whither show that he intends to push such questions only so far. The Transcendental articles of faith are paraded before the reader: "Behind nature, throughout nature, spirit is present: . . . spirit does not act upon us from without, that is, in space and time, but spiritually, or through ourselves" (*NAL,* p. 38). The point where Emerson stops short, as Carlyle would say, is the place where Carlyle himself foundered, where spirit and matter meet a common end, in death. Instead of plunging ahead into the abyss, like Carlyle, Emerson dances at the precipice. Only the Orphic poet — who is a Teufelsdröckhian "masquerade" in miniature introduced by Emerson in the last chapter — ventures a step or two further. "When men are innocent," the poet says, "life shall be longer, and shall pass into the immortal, as gently as we awake from dreams." Like Teufelsdröckh, the Orphic poet recognizes the inevitability of the cycle of destruction and rebirth; the world, he says, "is kept in check by death and infancy" (p. 42). But unlike Carlyle's fiction, Emerson's Transcendental masquerade allows him to entertain the dream of immortality without facing the nightmare of death.

Carlyle and Emerson had essentially completed their religious development by the time they reached their mid-thirties. Their speculations range over roughly the same terrain, with the same unmistakable landmarks. With a little indulgence, the metaphor may be stretched a bit further. Carlyle forged ahead relentlessly into undiscovered country and, in effect, vanished from the realm of religious speculation entirely. Emerson was content to pass his remaining forty years wandering in circles, and if he wandered the whole time in the same desert, at least it was a desert not utterly bereft of fruitful oases and even occasional visions from Mount Pisgah, whether mirages or not. This is not to suggest that he spent the rest of his life repeating himself. Like Carlyle, he developed other interests, and even in his later essays, lectures, and poems of a more or less Transcendental sort, he found an infinite variety of new approaches, new influences, and new directions. Tracing Emerson's further explorations lies outside our present scope. We have followed two spiritual wanderers in the hope of determining how far they traveled the same paths and where their courses began to diverge.

It is satisfying to suppose that one of the points of divergence first appeared at Craigenputtock in the attenuated discussion between the two young men on the subject of immortality. "Christ died on the tree; that built Dunscore kirk yonder; that brought you and me together. Time has only a relative existence." It will be recalled that at the time Emerson, who had recently lost his wife and left the ministry, was not overly pleased with this brief Orphic utterance. A little over two years later, in 1835, his emerging maturity is evident in a passage from a letter intended to console Carlyle for the accidental destruction of his *French Revolution* manuscript. "When you are weary," he told Carlyle, "believe, that you who stimulate virtuous young men, do not write a line in vain . . . To die of feeding the fires of others, were sweet; since it were not death, but self multiplication." But he caught himself immediately: "And yet, I like not the sound of what I have said, I who hold an orthodox substantial personal immortality" (L, p. 139). His transition from liberal Christian to Transcendentalist apparently was not yet complete.

What remained of Emerson's traditional religious convictions faded over the next few years in the process of composing the first documents of his mature thought. Now he could appreciate the significance of Carlyle's remark at Craigenputtock, and perhaps he could even understand why Carlyle could no longer abide with Transcendentalism. Emerson was now producing his own Transcendental observations on immortality and related topics, and he would continue to do so all his life. "Immortality," in fact, is the title of the closing selection in *Letters and Social Aims* (1875), the last book of essays to appear under Emerson's name. In a note to that essay, his son relates an anecdote: "In my youth I received this answer from my father, indirect yet none the less satisfying, when I asked him what he thought about a future life: 'We may be certain that, whatever it may be, no one will be disappointed' " (EW 8:438). Edward Emerson was satisfied despite the obvious grimness and even black humor he might have inferred from his father's answer. In his youth, the unsatisfactory answer to a similar question Emerson received from Carlyle was no less indirect, but it was not nearly so tough-minded.

In late 1835 Emerson wrote both the letter to Carlyle shakily affirming his belief in "personal immortality" and the journal entry critical of "Natural Supernaturalism." Time passed, and Emerson became a full-fledged Transcendentalist and speculative writer, like Carlyle. In October of 1837, Emerson dreamt one night of his own death. "I said when I awoke," he wrote in his journal: "After some more sleepings & wakings I shall lie on this mattrass sick; then, dead; and through my gay entry they will carry these bones. Where shall I be then?"[23] As he conceived an answer, his thoughts may well have strayed, if only for an instant, back to that cloudless day in Scotland. "I lifted my head," the entry continues, "and beheld the spotless orange light of the morning beaming up from the dark hills into the wide Universe." But perhaps he was merely repeating the ethereal promise of the Orphic poet, that we "shall pass into the immortal, as gently as we awake from dreams."

2

Self-Denial and Self-Reliance: Heroes and Representative Men

Emerson had to wait five years to receive compensation for his services as Carlyle's literary agent in America. In that time he had helped bring out several volumes of Carlyle's work beyond the original *Sartor Resartus,* including the first collection of his periodical essays. Emerson's "bibliopolic" activities, as the grateful Carlyle called them, involved striking deals and keeping accounts with various printers, papermakers, and booksellers, as well as editing and promoting. Until Carlyle's reputation became firmly established, Emerson occasionally had to guarantee notes and even borrow to meet expenses. But there was little Carlyle could do to further Emerson's career except pass around *Nature* and his printed orations and press him now and then for something more substantial. Finally, in 1841 Emerson sent to London his first series of *Essays.* Carlyle's publisher proposed an English edition with a preface by Carlyle, who at last would be able to send royalty payments in the other direction "to the man Emerson; saying: There, man! Tit for tat, the reciprocity *not* all on one side!" (L, p. 302).[1]

Carlyle's reaction to Emerson's book was warm and generous, at least initially. "Ah me," he wrote Emerson after reading it "all yesterday," "I felt as if in the wide world there were still but this one voice that responded intelligently to my own" (L, p. 295). As usual when he was discussing Emerson's work, Carlyle did not specify the sources of his admiration or discontent. He may have had particularly in mind a lengthy passage in "Self-Reliance," the second essay in the series, where Emerson with Carlylean sarcasm declares his independence from the "angry bigot" who "assumes this bountiful cause of Abolition" and the "foolish philanthropist" soliciting support for "miscellaneous popular charities; the education at college of fools; the building of meeting-houses to the vain end to which many now stand; alms to sots, and the thousand-fold Relief Societies" (EW 2:51-52). Carlyle relished such lists of fashionable quackeries, and in his preface to the English edition of the *Essays* he seized the opportunity to compile another of his own:

> Pleasures of Virtue, Progress of the Species, Black Emancipation, New Tarif, Eclecticism, Locofocoism, ghost of Improved-Socinianism: these with many other ghosts and substances are squeaking, jabbering, according to their capabilities, round this man; to one man among the sixteen millions' their jabber is all unmusical. The silent voices of the Stars above, and of the green Earth beneath, are profitabler to him . . . The words of such a man, what words he finds good to speak, are worth attending to. By degrees a small circle of living souls eager to hear is gathered. The silence of this man has to become speech: may this, too, in its due season, prosper for him!

Obviously, Carlyle was being wishful rather than commendatory; the little benediction is in fact the height of his praise for Emerson in the preface. At least Emerson was not a "squeaking, jabbering" Mammon-worshipper, corrupted by the "all-pervading jingle of dollars and loud chaffering of ambitions and promotions" in his "never-resting locomotive country." In exempting Emerson from the familiar American stereotype, Carlyle was expressing the hope that he might some day produce something of value; the implication that as yet he hadn't becomes explicit near the end: "What Emerson's talent is, we will not altogether estimate by this Book. The utterance is abrupt, fitful; the great idea not yet embodied struggles towards an embodiment."² As Joseph Slater suggests, Emerson's failure to mention this preface in his letter thanking Carlyle for the English *Essays* was probably an indication of his displeasure (L, p. 308).

The problem was that Emerson's essays are largely concerned with matters that Carlyle had pretty much lost interest in and had abandoned a decade earlier. Carlyle never categorically renounced the Transcendentalism of *Sartor Resartus* and his early periodical pieces, but the glow had already begun to fade by the time of Emerson's visit to Craigenputtock. Emerson must have quickly sensed—perhaps from Carlyle's florid but vaguely condescending reception of *Nature*—that Carlyle had changed his direction and that he would eventually be expected to follow. More explicitly, the experience of reading the long-awaited Divinity School Address, which had been lost in the mail for months, seems to have incited Carlyle to shake Emerson out of the Transcendental rut once and for all. "You tell us," he wrote,

> with piercing emphasis that man's soul is great; *shew* us a great soul of a man, in some work symbolic of such: this is the seal of such a message, and you will feel by and by that you are called to this. I long to see some concrete thing, some Event, Man's Life, American Forest, or piece of Creation, which this Emerson loves and wonders at, well *Emersonized:* depictured by Emerson, filled with the life of Emerson, and cast forth from him then to live by itself. If these Orations baulk me of this, how profitable soever they be for others, I will not love them. (L, p. 215)

He had become so aroused that he had to end the letter with an apology for his peremptory tone. "And yet what am I saying? How do I know what is good for *you?*"

But he continued to act as if he did know what was good for Emerson. When he took any notice at all, Emerson responded indirectly. After congratulating him on the success of the 1840 lecture series "On Heroes and Hero-Worship," he anticipated Carlyle's wish that he Emersonize some American heroes:

> We have our own problems to solve also & a good deal of movement & tendency emerging into sight every day in church & state, in social modes, & in letters. I sometimes fancy our cipher is larger & easier to read than that of your English society. You will naturally ask me if I try my hand in the history of all this, — I who have leisure and write? No, not in the near & practical way which they seem to invite. I incline to write philosophy, poetry, possibility, — anything but history. (L, p. 277)

Emerson was tacitly acknowledging the need for an American Carlyle and at the same time gently but decisively refusing to assume the position himself. This letter, incidentally, extended one of his many invitations to Carlyle to lecture in America. In addition to honest friendship, a tacit rejection of discipleship may underlie the endless invitations: instead of ordaining an American Carlyle, let Carlyle come to America. Not that Emerson would play the disciple even then: "Do not imagine," he had written in 1835, while extending the second invitation, "that I will hurt you in this unseen domain of yours by any Boswellism. Every suffrage you get here is fairly your own" (p. 120).

Whether or not he actually wanted Emerson for a disciple, Carlyle's longing for "some concrete thing" from Emerson remained long frustrated. While Carlyle was forwarding to Concord for American republication such books as *The French Revolution* (1837), *Heroes and Hero-Worship* (1841), *Past and Present* (1843), and *Cromwell* (1845), the only published writings Emerson could send to London were "these Orations" Carlyle refused to love, along with *Nature* and the two series of *Essays*. The English edition of the *Second Series* (1844) undertaken by Carlyle's publishers included from Carlyle only a brief notice warning readers away from unauthorized reprints. In a letter to Emerson, however, he asserted his disapproval of Emerson's whole manner. The new book, he said, was suitable as a sermon, even "a real *word,*" but

> For the rest, I have to object still (what you will call objecting against the Law of Nature) that we find you a Speaker, indeed, but as it were a *Soliloquizer* on the eternal mountain-tops only, in vast solitudes where men and their affairs lie all hushed in a very dim remoteness; and only *the man* and the stars and the earth are visible, —whom, so fine a fellow seems he, we could perpetually punch into, and say, "Why won't you come and help us then? We have terrible need of one man like you down among us! It is cold and vacant up there; nothing paintable but rainbows and emotions; come down and you shall do life-pictures, passions, facts . . . !"—To which he answers that he won't, can't, and doesn't want to (as the Cockneys have it): and so I leave him and say, "You Western Gymnosophist! Well, we can afford one man for that too. But—!" (pp. 370-371)

Emerson was understandably grateful to Carlyle for *not* writing another preface. "If you introduce me," he explained in his reply to Carlyle's letter, "your readers & the literary papers try to read me, & with false expectations. I had rather have fewer readers & only such as belong to me." That was diplomatic enough, but this time Emerson was really provoked, and he decided to meet head-on Carlyle's assault against his mountaintop solitude and rainbow-painting:

> But of what you say now & heretofore respecting the remoteness of my writing & thinking from real life, though I hear substantially the same criticism made by my countrymen, I do not know what it means. If I can at any time express the law & the ideal right, that should satisfy me without measuring the divergence from it of the last act of Congress. And though I sometimes accept a popular call, & preach on Temperance or the Abolition of slavery, as lately on the First of August, I am sure to feel before I have done with it, what an intrusion it is into another sphere & so much loss of virtue in my own. (p. 373)

After reading so heated a defense of spiritual isolationism, Carlyle could not have been terribly surprised to hear Emerson shortly afterwards apologetically admit to being a poet: "I sometimes write verses. I tell you with some unwillingness, as knowing your distaste for such things." But he added that he had recently written "a deal about Napoleon" and was now at work on other biographical subjects (p. 379). Carlyle was so pleased to see his distant friend turning in the right direction at last that in his letter back he forgave the poetry and heartily encouraged the projected biographies. He seemed to assume that his own *Heroes* book would serve as Emerson's model, and again he proposed that Emerson include an American subject. Emerson should "make an artistic bronze statue" of some "American Hero, one whom you really love" (p. 381). But Carlyle's hopes were quickly disappointed, for Emerson's next letter listed all the subjects (except Goethe) of his lecture series on "Representative Men," delivered in the winter of 1845-46. Although there were no Americans on the list, Carlyle was encouraged to think that Emerson at long last was coming down from the mountaintop.

Actually, Emerson had been down from the mountaintop for quite some time. Carlyle's notions about his solitude and isolation were, at least in part, misconceptions which Emerson failed to correct and to some extent may have deliberately fostered. For Carlyle, and for others who knew Emerson only through his published work, such misconceptions were to be expected, for most of his early publications were concerned with the speculative "rainbows and emotions" abhorred by the post-Transcendental Carlyle. A few pieces came nearer to the "concrete things" and "life-pictures" Carlyle wanted; he especially admired "The American Scholar" (1837), which "went tingling thro' my heart" and drew from Jane Carlyle a comparison with Schiller (L, p. 173). Nevertheless, his published writings through the 1840s on the whole did not belie Carlyle's impression of Emerson as "a *Soliloquizer* on the eternal mountain-tops." But Emerson did not publish everything he wrote.

For one thing, he kept voluminous journals and notebooks, which are crammed with reflections upon practically every aspect of the world around him. Journals, however, are private affairs; hermits on mountaintops are perfectly capable of keeping up-to-date journals. Of greater importance are his lectures, for after his resignation from the ministry in 1832, Emerson was a professional lecturer. When Carlyle in 1839 urged him to "*shew* us the great soul of a man" rather than speculate on the nature of the soul, he had forgotten that four years earlier Emerson had told him of giving "some Biographical Lectures, which were meant for theories or portraits of Luther, Michelangelo, Milton, George Fox, Burke" (p. 122). Had Carlyle been better informed about the extent and quality of Emerson's lectures in the thirties and early forties, his conception of him would surely have been different. The mere titles of some of them, individual lectures and whole courses, would have convinced Carlyle that his interests were "concrete" as well as speculative: "English Literature" (1835-36), "The Philosophy of History" (1836-37), "The Present Age" (1839-40), "Man the Reformer" (1841), "Lectures on the Times" (1841-42). Admittedly, the contents of Emerson's lectures are often more ethereal than the titles, but it should also be remembered that he had to choose topics which would attract paying audiences. Carlyle's knowledge of these lectures generally was limited to what he could learn from Emerson's letters, since many of them were not published during either man's lifetime.[3] Emerson usually provided Carlyle with little more than the subjects, if that much; occasionally, in the hope of enticing Carlyle to lecture in America himself, he offered some details of the lecturer's life. He never discussed the substance of his lectures, though doing so would have allayed Carlyle's distress over his remoteness.

It is conceivable that Emerson intentionally cultivated the role of reclusive dreamer in his correspondence with Carlyle.

In his second letter, written soon after his move from the Boston area to Concord in the fall of 1834, he answered Carlyle's request that he tell something about himself:

> Account me "a drop in the ocean seeking another drop," or God-ward, striving to keep so true a sphericity as to receive the due ray from every point of the concave heaven. Since my return home, I have been left very much at leisure. It were long to tell all my speculations upon my profession & my doings thereon; but, possessing my liberty, I am determined to keep it at the risk of uselessness . . . until such duties offer themselves as I can with integrity discharge. (p. 109)

The truth is that at the time Emerson had already the previous spring completed his first course of lectures, on natural history. But he knew that Carlyle retained a romanticized picture of him from the Craigenputtock visit; in his first letter, which led to the misty self-description above, Carlyle recalled his "supernal character," "so pure and still, with intent so charitable; and then vanishing too so soon into the azure Inane, as an Apparition should" (p. 101). In subsequent letters Emerson continued to dwell on his "leisure" and "liberty" even "at the risk of uselessness" — almost to the point of morally justifying uselessness. In his letter responding to Carlyle's criticism of the second *Essays* volume, it will be recalled, he admitted to speaking "sometimes" on issues such as temperance and abolition, insisting that such lapses were an "intrusion" and a "loss of virtue." He was perfectly aware that abolition and temperance were of little interest to Carlyle, who much preferred history, literature, and biography — the very subjects Emerson indeed had been speaking on for years, often rather than "sometimes." Carlyle himself reluctantly delivered four courses of public lectures in those fields between 1837 and 1840; yet it was Carlyle, not Emerson, who first suggested that perhaps their work as lecturers had something in common. "Curious," he wrote in 1838, "your Course of Lectures 'on Human Culture' seems to be on the very subject I am to discourse upon here in May coming; but I am to call it 'on the History of Literature.' " Emerson ignored the hint in his reply; instead he lovingly described his house and property in Concord, his financial security, his leisure to "sit & read & write with very little system." And he invited the Carlyles to come join him for a year (pp. 182-185).

Emerson's evocation of the pastoral serenity of Concord touches upon another submerged conflict between the two men. When they first met, the roles of rustic and urbanite had been reversed. The Carlyles' isolated farmhouse at Craigenputtock, along with what he learned of the peasant background of its master, aroused the sympathies of the native Bostonian, and after the visit, the romantic image of a fearless visionary living in wholesome poverty in the remote countryside may have mitigated in Emerson's mind the disappointment of the actual meeting. In the letter to Alexander Ireland in which he expressed doubts about Carlyle's intellectual power, he also wrote of Carlyle: "I am afraid he finds his solitude tedious, but I could not help congratulating him upon his treasure in his wife & I hope they will not leave the moors. Tis so much better for a man of letters to nurse himself in seclusion than to be filed down to the common level by the compliances & imitations of city society."[4] Similarly, in his first letter to Carlyle, he spoke of "the favored condition of my lonely philosopher" and recalled "sitting upon one of your broad hills." Carlyle's sensitivity to Emerson's romantic recollections is apparent in the pains he took to justify his removal to London in his first letter to Emerson. "Yes, my friend," he confessed, "it is even so: Craigenputtock now stands solitary in the wilderness . . . Censure not; I came to London for the best of all reasons: To seek bread and work." He recognized that he was now in a "strange element" in which he was "as good as an Alien." He assured Emerson he would not be corrupted: "I care not for Radicalism, for Toryism, for Church, Tithes or the 'Confusion' of Useful Knowledge: much as I can speak and hear, I am alone, alone" (pp. 104-105).

Despite the echoing lamentation of his continued loneliness even in the heart of the city, the news of Carlyle's changed environment probably renewed Emerson's apprehensions. But in his next letter to Carlyle, the first from Concord, he obediently refrained from censuring the move to London, except perhaps by not commenting upon it at all. Each man had retained a romatic image of the other from their meeting in Scotland; only Emerson tried to keep the illusion about himself alive.

The time has come to draw some conclusions and in the process to retrace some old ground. I have suggested that Emerson's disillusionment with Carlyle began at Craigenputtock. Along with the inevitable disenchantment of a young man who meets for the first time someone he admires, he was disturbed by Carlyle's stubborn reticence on religious and speculative matters and consequently grew skeptical of his capacity for true depth of thought. But he still respected him for his courage and integrity, and he left Europe with a personal affection for the lonely couple on the Scottish moors. The following year he was sufficiently impressed by the early installments of *Sartor Resartus* to renew the acquaintance by mail, although a lingering distrust of Carlyle's profundity caused him to read the philosophical novel more critically than if the two men had never met. His criticisms had no effect on Carlyle, who had by now finished with Teufelsdröckh and Transcendentalism and had little interest in or sympathy with works of that nature, including the writings Emerson himself soon began to publish. For his part, Emerson probably came to regard Carlyle's abandonment of Transcendentalism for history, politics, and biography as all of a piece with his desertion of tranquil Craigenputtock for the cacophony of London. As it happened, Emerson had moved in the precise opposite geographical direction, to Concord. In the face of Carlyle's exhortations to join him in his commitment to reality and immediacy, Emerson consistently portrayed himself, in the letters and writings he sent to Carlyle, as the remote philosopher whose dedication to the highest truths outweighs his concern with the practical affairs of his fellow beings.

Emerson deliberately underplayed his lectures in his letters to Carlyle in an effort to establish an independent identity in Carlyle's eyes and in the eyes of others. Many of his friends, as well as enemies like Andrews Norton, already regarded him merely as a disciple of the earlier, "Kantian" Carlyle, and it may have occurred to him that Carlyle, too, thought of him in the same way. As it was, a review of Emerson by an acquaintance of Carlyle, Richard Monckton Milnes, which appeared in 1840 in the *London and Westminster Review*, faintly praised him for possessing "a mind cognate to" Carlyle's, "however inferior in energies and influences."[5] Although he had reservations about the article, Carlyle told Emerson that it might serve as "the first plank of a kind of pulpit for you here and throughout all Saxondom," and he had Milnes send him a copy (L, p. 264). Emerson countered with an apologetically defensive letter to Milnes. "I told him," he explained to Carlyle, "that if I should print more he would find me worse than ever" because his journals were "full of disjointed dreams, audacities, unsystematic irresponsible lampoons of systems, and all manner of rambling reveries" (p. 272).

Had Carlyle learned that Emerson had in fact "followed" him into such fields as history and biography, then Emerson would have had still greater reason to fear becoming forever known as just another of Carlyle's disciples. After the success of his two volumes of *Essays*, he could watch his own reputation grow in Britain as well as in America, weakening the tendency in both countries to label him a disciple of anyone. By the time he began to prepare the "Representative Men" lectures in the mid-1840s, he had enough confidence to write about the project to Carlyle. Even so, he delayed publication till 1850, that is, until he had delivered the lectures in England during his second European visit. "I learn that your Boston Lectures have been attended with renown enough," Carlyle wrote in 1846, before the idea for a speaking tour in Britain had even been proposed; "When are the lectures themselves to get to print?" (p. 393). The unarticulated answer was: not until he had a chance to speak them personally before Carlyle's countrymen. Yet the desire to step outside Carlyle's shadow was not the only reason for Emerson's hesitation about publishing.

As earnest writers whose speculative fancies had ended in a perception of unbreachable limitation, leaving them, perhaps, with some sense of futility and metaphysical uneasiness, history and biography were reasonable areas in which to redirect their energies. In the great works of their youth, *Sartor Resartus* and *Nature*, Carlyle and Emerson struggled with the final questions beyond life and death: whence and whither; they discovered either that there are no answers to these questions or, what amounts to the same thing, that the answers, like the questions, are nothing more than so many words. And words have meaning only as a part of human life, and only in the course of human life can questions be meaningfully asked and answered. Instead of telling us that the soul is great, Carlyle chided Emerson, "*shew* us a great soul of a man." And in 1840 Carlyle took his own advice and publicly exhibited the great souls of heroes. A few years later Emerson even more explicitly declared biography the legitimate heir of theology: "The questions of Whence? What? and Whither?" he wrote in *Representative Men*, "and the solution of these must be in a life, and not in a book" (EW 4:94). (Ironically, this statement appears in the chapter on Swedenborg, whose mystical ideas had influenced Emerson's own Transcendentalism.)

To say that the emphasis shifted from heaven to earth, or from the soul to the self, does not mean that either Carlyle or Emerson abruptly transferred his entire literary enterprise into a completely different mode, like a former golfer taking up tennis. A man's intellectual development is never that simple. Both men, in fact, had a longstanding interest in biography. Carlyle served his apprenticeship writing un-

signed encyclopedia articles on biographical subjects; his
first published book, aside from the translation of *Wilhelm
Meister's Apprenticeship*, was a *Life of Schiller* (1825).
Emerson's taste for biography had begun to develop with a
childhood love of Plutarch, and, as we have seen, biography
was the subject of one of his first courses of lectures. Each
man probably had formed many of his essential beliefs on
human conduct, as well as his conception of the self, long
before hearing of Transcendentalism. And each man's
theory of the self underlies the manner in which he practices
the art of biography.

Their ideas of the self turn upon two ancient problems:
good and evil, and freedom and necessity. Since they perceived these problems in terms of ethics rather than metaphysics, their positions were relatively unaffected by the
collapse of their faith in Christian metaphysics and their
subsequent Transcendental experiments, for they continued
to regard much of Christian ethics as still intact, though now
inescapably secular. It never seems to have occurred to them
to question their ethical convictions merely because they
had discarded all supernatural justification for them. In
other words, it would be premature to call Carlyle and
Emerson existentialists.

Despite the continuity between Christian and Transcendental ethics, however, neither Carlyle nor Emerson can be
said to have reverted from Transcendentalism to a
truncated form of Christianity. Anglo-American Transcendentalism unsuccessfully attempted to redefine the Christian soul. Abandonment of the soul led to a renewed emphasis on the secular self, resulting, among other things, in
an ever greater commitment to history and biography. And
while it is true that vestiges of Christian belief survive in
their biographical and historical writings, particularly with
regard to ethics, it is still misleading to describe either man
as a Christian or even as a "secular Christian." An even
more problematic label is "Puritan," which has a limited
applicability, especially for Carlyle, but which often pro-

duces unlimited confusion because of the multiple conno-
tations and emotional baggage that the term carries.

Carlyle was memorably described by his biographer,
James Anthony Froude, as "a Calvinist without the theology." Those words reappear in many books about Carlyle
because they seem to imply a vast and significant truth
without really saying anything of substance. Taken literally,
the catchy phrase reduces to little more than meaningless
self-contradiction, like the joke about *Hamlet* without the
Prince of Denmark. An equally empty modern variation of
Froude's formula refers to Carlyle's "Puritan temperament"
or "Calvinist prejudices" and "instincts." Of course, it is undeniable that Carlyle's personality, predisposition, *Weltan-
schauung*, or whatever was deeply and permanently marked
by the Puritan beliefs and religious practices to which he
was exposed from birth. It is also true that he abandoned
but never entirely disowned the dissenting creed of his childhood; furthermore, until her death in 1854, when he was
nearly sixty, his mother acted as a living and often vocal reminder of the claims of his Puritan background upon him.
But such influences, if that is the word, operate mysteriously
and their effects are all but intangible. Certainly, there is no
evidence that he ever returned to his family's faith in any
meaningful sense; nor did he ever assent to any other organized form of religious practice.[6] And the same was true of
Emerson.

Although Emerson's Unitarian background was quite
different, all his life he took great pride in the stern
spirituality of his own Puritan ancestors. As with Carlyle
and his mother, he had a long-lived reminder of his Puritan
heritage in the person of his Calvinist Aunt Mary, who ex-
erted a strong influence on his largely fatherless youth and
who boldly promoted her religion against his Unitarianism
as well as his later Transcendentalism. While no one would
call Emerson "a Calvinist without the theology," it would
not be unreasonable to speak of his sharing with Carlyle to
some degree a "Puritan temperament."[7] As we shall see

shortly, Carlyle and Emerson engaged in a half-serious debate, provoked by their disagreement over Goethe, about
who was the more "Puritanical." "Believe me," Carlyle was
moved to exclaim at one point,"it is impossible you can be
more a Puritan than I; nay I often feel as if I were far too
much so" (L, p. 114).

Analyzing such matters as the conception of the self on
the basis of either writer's "Puritanism," whether of the theological or "temperamental" variety, is a hazardous undertaking, yielding questionable results of limited value in
determining the actual substance of their thought. Two
concepts associated with Calvinism, inherent human depravity and arbitrary predestination, obviously have some
bearing on the crucial issues of good and evil, and freedom
and necessity; yet each man can be held as a proponent of
both "Calvinist" and "anti-Calvinist" positions on both
questions. Carlyle's preoccupation with evil, I suppose, may
derive ultimately from the Calvinist doctrine of helpless human depravity, while Emerson's strain of fatalism often
seems vaguely predestinarian. Those who find such analo-
gies useful are welcome to bear them in mind. For our present purpose, which is to examine the philosophical foundations of their work in biography, primarily, the best
approach is to allow them to speak in their own terms, which
are confusing enough without introducing extraneous com-
plications.

The terms most characteristic of Carlyle and Emerson
when they discuss the self are "self-denial" and "self-reliance." The latter, of course, is linked inextricably with
Emerson; in free association the term would almost invariably elicit the name. Carlyle throughout his life spoke of
self-denial, using that particular word along with a number
of others, in German and English, which he considered
more or less equivalent to self-denial, regardless of their
original significance. Such terms include "Renunciation"
(*Entsagen*) from Goethe, "Annihilation of Self" (*Selbsttödt-
ung*) from Novalis, and "Divine Depth of Sorrow," "Wor-

ship of Sorrow," and the like from traditional Christian rhetoric.[8] On the surface, Carlyle's term and Emerson's sound mutually antagonistic and would seem to lead to mutually antagonistic positions on the problems of good and evil and of freedom and fate. Self-denial might imply the essential evil of the self, demanding in turn a denial of freedom in order to keep that evil in check. Self-reliance, on the other hand, suggests a virtuous self for which the greatest freedom would yield the greatest good. But as is often the case, the simplicity of the terms belies the intricacy of the ideas which the labels are supposed to identify.

The focus of Carlyle's approach to good and evil is his vision of an insatiable self. Because human thirsts are unquenchable, man is doomed to unhappiness no matter how hard he tries to satisfy his desires. Had Carlyle been a true "Calvinist," he would then have concluded that as a consequence of man's insatiability the human condition must always result in evil, unless divine grace rescued man from his innate depravity. But Carlyle's infinitely yearning self is a force for goodness, even for greatness, as well as for evil. It is significant that in *Sartor Resartus* Teufelsdröckh's exposition of the "Origin of Evil" and the nature of human unhappiness occurs not in the despairing, suicidal "Everlasting No" chapter, but as part of the affirmative "Everlasting Yea." Although he regards evil in the traditional manner as a consequence of human selfishness, he also suggests that from that same self-centered impulse arise man's infinite aspirations:

> Man's Unhappiness, as I construe, comes of his Greatness; it is because there is an Infinite in him, which with all his cunning he cannot quite bury under the Finite. Will the whole Finance Ministers and Upholsterers and Confectioners of modern Europe undertake, in joint-stock company, to make one Shoeblack HAPPY? They cannot accomplish it, above an hour or two: for the Shoeblack has also a Soul quite other than his Stomach; and would require, if you consider it, for his per-

manent satisfaction and saturation, simply this allotment, and no less: *God's infinite Universe altogether to himself,* therein to enjoy infinitely, and fill every wish as fast as it rose. Oceans of Hochheimer, a Throat like that of Ophiuchus: speak not of them; to the infinite Shoeblack they are as nothing. No sooner is your ocean filled, than he grumbles that it might have been of better vintage. Try him with half a Universe, of an Omnipotence, he sets to quarrelling with the proprietor of the other half, and declares himself the most maltreated of men. — Always there is a black spot in our sunshine: it is even, as I said, the *Shadow of Ourselves. (SR,* p. 190)

In this remarkable passage, Carlyle's Everyman — in nineteenth-century fashion a shoeblack rather than a rustic — displays an unmistakable longing to replace God, a desire which Carlyle deplores as the source of unhappiness but at the same time exalts as the will to greatness. The shoeblack is both gluttonous and heroic, both a depraved wine guzzler and a type of Christ, who also had to bury his infinite under the finite. Good and evil, it would appear, are relative, even comparable qualities: what they have in common is strength of will. John Sterling, a shrewd inquisitor of Carlyle's various heresies, interpreted his frequent citation of Goethe's aphorism on the "shadow of ourselves" along these same lines. "I find in all my conversations with B.," Sterling wrote in a letter, referring to Carlyle, "that his fundamental position is, the good of evil: he is for ever quoting Goethe's epigram about the idleness of wishing to jump off one's shade." In his *Life of Sterling* Carlyle dismissed his young friend's observation as "indicating conversations on the Origin of Evil, or rather resolution on my part to suppress such, as wholly fruitless and worthless; which are now all grown dark to me!" Carlyle's plea of faulty memory is somewhat disingenuous, for in private conversation Sterling often must have pressed him to clarify his ideas beyond the level of meaning that initially satisfied him.[9]

He did not always develop his model of the self in the

even-handed manner of the *Sartor* passage, where the animal appetite for "Oceans of Hochheimer" and the mystic longing for "God's infinite Universe" are almost equal expressions of the human drive for greatness. More commonly he emphasized the spiritual pole of desire over the physical, but he never condemned man's animal appetites as evil in themselves.

"Our feelings are in favour of heroism," he wrote in his first book, the *Life of Schiller*; "We *wish* to be pure and perfect" (CW 25:195). Some fifteen years before *Heroes and Hero-Worship*, Carlyle's theory of human greatness thus appeared in miniature, though recognizable only in retrospect. Sometimes he justified spiritual ambition, the wish to be "pure and perfect," through images of physical expansion, as in the familiar passage in his first essay on Richter where Carlyle defended peculiarities in literary style by citing the "great law of culture." Everyone should strive to realize his full potential because "all *genuine* things are what they ought to be." For example, the "reindeer is good and beautiful, so likewise is the elephant." Perhaps the elephant reminded him of the human proboscis, for the passage goes on to consider "noses of wonderful dimensions" which cannot "justly be amputated by the public, —not even the nose of Slawkenbergius himself; so it *be* a real nose, and no wooden one put on for deception's sake and mere show!" (CW 26:19). The animals and Slawkenbergius's nose are only playful illustrations, but their presence reflects his fundamental conviction that all human capacities and aspirations participate in a universal thrust towards greatness. In relation to the self, even good and evil in a sense are part of the total process of aspiration rather than a question of absolute, irreconcilable choices. "Morality itself," he asked in *Heroes and Hero-Worship*, "what we call the moral quality of a man, what is this but another *side* of the one vital Force whereby he is and works" (CW 5:106).

This moral relativism reflects his peculiar (but not, in my opinion, perverse) attitude toward happiness. To be sure, he

valued good over evil, and happiness over misery. Nevertheless, he instinctively preferred activity and expansion, regardless of the benefits or consequences in terms of morality
and happiness, over passivity and contraction or self-satis-
fied stability. The Everyman-Shoeblack in *Sartor Resartus*
was allowed an infinite appetite of the stomach as well as the
soul, but neither can ever be completely satisfied. The inevitable unhappiness is commendable, because it can lead
to greatness; at the very least it incites to action. More than
anything he detested the mere passive reception of whatever
one is given rather than the active quest for what one desires, no matter how unattainable.

Shortly after disposing of the shoeblack, Teufelsdröckh
examines his own unhappiness and wonders if the reason for
it is "Because the THOU (sweet gentleman) is not sufficiently honoured, nourished, soft-bedded, and lovingly
cared-for?" He then asks, "What if thou wert born and predestined not to be Happy, but to be Unhappy! Art thou
nothing other than a Vulture, then, that fliest through the
Universe seeking after somewhat to *eat*; and shrieking dole-
fully because carrion enough is not given thee?" (*SR*, pp.
191-192). The passive construction underscores the cow-
ardly acquiescence Carlyle is denouncing, including the
passive acceptance of fate. The part about predestination
does not counsel man to resign himself to being unhappy,
but on the contrary exhorts him to take action whether he is
predestined to unhappiness or not. Teufelsdröckh answers
the question What if thou art born to be unhappy? at the
end of the paragraph with the formula: "Close thy *Byron*;
open thy *Goethe*." For Carlyle, "Byronism" means gloomy
but impotent rebellion against destiny; in effect, Byron's
melancholy dissatisfaction is identical with passive resignation because the result of both attitudes is inaction. Thus
Professor Teufelsdröckh, lecturing on heroism in the article
"Goethe's Works" (1832), relates as an example of
"Self-Worship" an anecdote in which Byron sulks over being
given a plain bun instead of a spiced bun. "His bun,"
Teufelsdröckh comments, "was a life-rent of God's universe,

with the tasks it offered, and the tools to do them with" (CW 27:397). It is not that Byron should be happy with whatever he is given, but his dissatisfaction should cause him to strive to make the most of whatever he can get. Conversely, Goethe stands for activity, simply to "Do the Duty which lies nearest thee," despite unhappiness and in the teeth of necessity. On one level, Carlyle is praising the mere act of working, the very process of labor for its own sake, as opposed to doing nothing and parasitically waiting to be served by others, like Byron sulking over his buns. In this sense, Carlyle may be seen as a supporter of the "Protestant work ethic" as explicated by R. H. Tawney, or, paradoxically, as a proto-Marxist anticipating the philosophical ramifications of the labor theory of value.[10] And his ideas may well have unforeseen implications in economics as well as in other fields. But at bottom the essence of his plea for endless activity and expansion against passivity and resignation is a vital commitment to freedom of the will against the inevitability of fate. The struggle between freedom and necessity lies at the heart of his theory of the self and ultimately animates his practice of the art of biography.

In an article called "Biography" (1832), designed as part of an essay on Boswell's *Life of Johnson*, he divides the appeal of biography into two components:

A scientific interest and a poetic one alike inspire us in this matter. A scientific: because every mortal has a Problem of Existence set before him, which, were it only, what for the most it is, the Problem of keeping soul and body together, must be to a certain extent *original,* unlike every other; and yet, at the same time, so *like* every other; like our own, therefore; instructive, moreover, since we also are indentured to *live.* A poetic interest still more: for precisely this same struggle of human Freewill against material Necessity, which every man's Life, by the mere circumstance that the man continues alive, will more or less victoriously exhibit, — is that which above all else, or rather inclusive of all else, calls the Sympathy of mortal hearts into action. (CW 28:44-45)

The "scientific" and "poetic" aspects of biography correspond significantly, though subtly, with the two crises of Teufelsdröckh's conversion experience in *Sartor Resartus*. In "The Everlasting No," Teufelsdröckh overcomes his Wertherian impulse toward suicide and conquers his fear of death; in the language of the "Biography" essay, he solves his "Problem of Existence" by deciding that, after all, he is "indentured to live," even without hope. The chapter ends when his "whole Me" tells the Everlasting No: "*I* am not thine, but Free, and forever hate thee!" In "The Everlasting Yea," his freedom confronts the specter of destiny, the possibility that he was "born and predestined not to be Happy, but to be Unhappy." In terms of "Biography," he enlists on the side of "human Freewill" against the "material Necessity" which may well have predestined him to misery. The struggle is universal, and the self, simply by virtue of being alive and being human, must fight on the side of freedom against fate.

Therefore self-denial cannot have meant to Carlyle denial of the freedom of the self. His social theories (which I will take up later) may tend toward a form of historical determinism, but emotionally at least he always remained in sympathy with the idea of personal free will. He had a strong commitment to the reality of evil, but he refused to ascribe evil to the infinite aspirations of the self, even in the case of a figure from the past whose actions are known to have been unjust and wrong. Near the end of "Biography" he exclaimed with passion (and in his own voice rather than through his Germanic persona for the occasion, "Professor Gottfried Sauerteig") that "even they that were base and wicked while alive" are somehow redeemed now that they are dead. "Their baseness and wickedness was not *They*, was but the heavy and unmanageable Environment that lay round them, with which they fought unprevailing: *they* (the ethereal god-given Force that dwelt in them, and was their *Self*) have now shuffled-off that heavy Environment, and are free and pure; their life-long Battle, go how it might, is all ended" (CW 28:56). The human essence is both free and good. One of the ways the great man differs from everyone else is in his greater ability to overcome his environment rather than be defeated or perverted by it, but the difference is of degree rather than of kind. Everyone, from Teufelsdröckh's shoeblack to the greatest hero, can claim as a birthright boundless freedom for self-realization.

Self-denial means renouncing self-satisfaction in favor of infinite expansion of the ideal self. Self-denial also means to assert freedom against necessity, to try to overcome human limitations, and to attempt to seize omnipotence, however hopeless the aspiration.

Emerson's theory of the self has much in common with Carlyle's. In *Representative Men* he even matches Teufelsdröckh's infinite shoeblack with a parable of his own on the "young and ardent minds" who grieve over "the incompetency of power."

> They accuse the divine Providence of a certain parsimony. It has shown the heaven and earth to every child and filled him with a desire for the whole; a desire raging, infinite; a hunger, as of space to be filled with planets; a cry of famine, as of devils for souls. Then for the satisfaction, — to each man is administered a single drop, a bead of dew of vital power, *per day,* — a cup as large as space, and one drop of the water of life in it. Each man woke in the morning with an appetite that could eat the solar system like a cake; a spirit for action and passion without bounds; he could lay his hand on the morning star; he could try conclusions with gravitation or chemistry; but, on the first motion to prove his strength, — hands, feet, senses, gave way and would not serve him . . . In every house, in the heart of each maiden and of each boy, in the soul of the soaring saint, this chasm is found, — between the largest promise of ideal power, and the shabby experience. (EW 4:184-185)[11]

The Emersonian Everyman also possesses an infinite self with gargantuan appetites expanding in every conceivable direction. He, too, could eat the solar system for breakfast (no doubt washing it all down with oceans of Hochheimer) or aspire to the stars. And again, the gap between ambition and achievement inevitably produces unhappiness, "the shabby experience."

The difference between them, however, is crucial: Emerson did not share Carlyle's commitment to freedom of the will. In *Freedom and Fate* Stephen E. Whicher dramatically narrates the movement of Emerson's thought from "revolution" to "acquiescence and optimism." The journey is complete in the essay on "Fate" in *The Conduct of Life* (1860); there, Whicher argues, Emerson no longer claims the "total freedom" of his youth, but now realizes that "freedom, like everything else in human life, is limited and partial; behind it, including it, is necessity."[12] *Freedom and Fate* speaks admirably for itself, but there is a general rule in Emerson studies that evidence can always be found to contradict the most carefully considered conclusions. As it happens, one of the many instances of apparent fatalism in Emerson's early life can be found in his first letter to Carlyle, where he wrote elegantly of "all our circlets of will as so many little eddies rounded in by the great circle of Necessity." It is my belief that a far more significant strain of youthful fatalism is perceptible, paradoxically enough, in his great declaration of individual freedom, the essay "Self-Reliance."

"What is the aboriginal Self," he asks in "Self-Reliance," "on which a universal reliance may be grounded?" In answering his question, he first differentiates conscious thought from "Spontaneity or Instinct"—yet another variation of the Transcendental epistemology. But whereas previously he and Carlyle had proclaimed the superiority of intuition primarily to refute the logic of materialism, here Emerson seeks to establish the overwhelming power of forces which lie beyond the control of the will and outside conscious awareness; in other words, he wants to make the Kantian reason absolute. As he proceeds to speak of "the fountain of action and of thought" and "the lungs of that inspiration which giveth man wisdom," what he describes may be called God or necessity, but whatever the name, it dominates the human will. It "cannot be denied without impiety or atheism" because everyone is reliant upon it, knowingly or not, voluntarily or not. The passivity of self-reliance follows from man's utter dependence for all vital power on a force that acts on the passive self from outside: self-reliance, it has been said, is "God-reliance."[13] "We lie in the lap of immense intelligence," the essay continues, "which makes us receivers of its truth and organs of its activity. When we discern justice, when we discern truth, we do nothing of ourselves, but allow a passage to its beams." Only these "involuntary perceptions" are important, and they must be accepted with "a perfect faith." An act of the will (as if there were really anything of significance left for the will to act upon) can only be "roving" or a mere "notion." What truly matters in human affairs is determined by a "perception" that "is not whimsical, but fatal" (EW 2:64-65).

If the truth of the universe must be perceptible to all, then an act in violation of that truth would be conceivable only in the absence of free will; otherwise one would be violating one's own nature. Carlyle could not declare the power of the reason absolute in this sense because he sought to preserve a limitless realm for the free expansion of human possibility. Thus he asserted freedom of the will even against a perception of necessity, while Emerson made the perception of necessity the very means for negating freedom of the will.

Carlyle and Emerson were men of ideas as well as men of letters, but they were never ideologues, and there is no reason to interpret their biographical and historical writings as illustrations of abstract concepts or theories, whether Transcendental or of some other variety. As biographers, they had a genuine interest in the people about whom they chose to write, and in their better work they displayed the

knack of all skillful biographers to make their subjects come
alive. Their philosophical ideas and attitudes acted as
undercurrents, creating waves but rarely breaking the surface.

Some efforts to differentiate their biographical practices
are plausible enough but shallow and misleading. Thoreau,
who regarded Carlyle and Emerson as "the complement of
each other," distinguished Carlyle's sympathy with "men of
action" from Emerson's preference for "thinkers."[14]
Thoreau's "broad and rude distinction" is obviously right
and obviously wrong; both authors wrote about active and
contemplative subjects. Another distinction, of greater
depth but more misleading, contrasts the two men politically, opposing Emerson's "democratic cult of greatness" (to
borrow a phrase from Stephen Whicher) to Carlyle's
attitude, which is usually, though not invariably, considered
more elitist or authoritarian. The political biases of biographers necessarily color their work, especially with portraits of "great men," but the main concern of good biography is a particular person, and not politics.

In any case we should resist the temptation to use protean
words like "democracy" and "equality" as shibboleths to
divide instantly and permanently one writer from the other.
The egalitarianism of *Representative Men* is most explicit in
the final part of the opening chapter, "Uses of Great Men,"
where Emerson questions the value of great men vis-à-vis
"the masses." If he is responding directly to Carlyle's book,
which seems likely, he is attacking hero worship rather than
heroism. "Why are the masses," he asks, "from the dawn of
history down, food for knives and powder? The idea digni-
fies a few leaders . . . but what for the wretches whom they
hire and kill?" His answer rejects the notion that most
people are inferior to some people: "there are no common
men. All men are at last of a size . . . Ask the great man if
there be none greater. His companions are." History itself
becomes "democratic," the collective achievement of all,
not the accomplishments of a few. "The genius of humanity

is the real subject whose biography is written in our annals" (EW 4: 30-32).

Heroes and Hero-Worship offers a different theory of history. "Universal History," Carlyle explains in his opening lecture, "is at bottom the History of the Great Men who have worked here." Not only are his heroes the "leaders" and "modellers" of the masses; they are even "in a wide sense creators of what soever the general mass of men contrived to do or to attain" (CW 5:1). He seems to be on the other end of the scale from Emerson, but Emerson is capable of sounding precisely the same note. In "Self-Reliance" he equates "all history" with "the biography of a few stout and earnest persons" (EW 2:61). And Carlyle, on the other hand, in the article "On History" (1830), proposes a definition of history fully in tune with Emerson's egalitarianism: "Social Life is the aggregate of all the individual men's Lives who constitute society; History is the essence of innumerable Biographies" (CW 27:86). To confuse matters further, in *his* essay on "History" Emerson advances a conclusion that might be read either way: "There is properly no history, only biography" (EW 2:9-10).

Much of the confusion among these clashing historical theories arises from imprecise terminology rather than from real contradiction. Philip Rosenberg's resolution of the dilemma for Carlyle is equally applicable to Emerson: "The idea that history should be the biography of great men and the idea that it should be the essence of the biographies 'of all the individual men . . . who constitute society' were alternative forms of the same truth."[15] The "elitist" Carlyle would no more characterize humanity as a mass of sheep with an occasional shepherd than would the "democratic" Emerson suggest that all should be chiefs and none should be braves. The titles of their books deserve much of the blame for such misconceptions. *Heroes and Hero-Worship* is a particularly unfortunate title from a twentieth-century perspective. The words can easily conjure a hideous two-headed monstrosity, with some popular vision of Nietzsche's

Übermensch facing down some Nazi fiction of an *Unter-mensch*. Carlyle had nothing of the sort in mind, nor did he even intend his two terms to be taken as antitheses. He wanted everyone to recognize and follow great men not for the glory of the hero but to overcome the paralysis of with-drawing into oneself. Hero worship, like heroism, was for Carlyle an expression of self-denial. The true hero was worthy of worship or emulation because of his greater self-denial. Hero and hero worshipper were engaged in the same undertaking; their roles were mutually supportive and per-haps, as Rosenberg shrewdly suggests, even interchangeable in a sense.[16] Carlyle's hero might well agree with Emerson's great man that their "companions" are greater.

Emerson also encouraged emulation of great men, not in pursuit of self-denial, but for the opposite purpose of self-aggrandizement. As he explained in *Representative Men*, because everyone is "self-defended," emulation of others will never lead to self-surrender: "You are you, and I am I, and so we remain" (EW 4:28). His answer to hero worship is im-plicit in the title of his opening chapter, "Uses of Great Men." The great man should be *used*; he is not worthy of being worshipped merely for his power, since the power he possesses, like the power anyone possesses, does not come from an act of the will. The great man does not even deserve the gratitude of those his greatness benefits, for "all mental and moral force . . . goes out from you, whether you will or not, and profits me whom you never thought of" (pp. 13-14). Neither great thoughts nor great actions are attrib-utable to volition. "The power which they communicate is not theirs. When we are exalted by ideas, we do not owe this to Plato, but to the idea, to which also Plato was debtor" (p. 19). The words "representative men," especially in com-parison with the title of Carlyle's book, sound very demo-cratic, like the lower house of Congress, but democracy had little to do with the forces Emerson's representative men actually represented. "He is great who is what he is from na-ture" (p. 6).[17] In the same way, Carlyle's distaste for democracy had little to do with the heroism of his heroes or the reverence of the heroes' worshippers.

Emerson's determination to withhold from the great man the responsibility for his greatness clearly contradicts Carlyle, who was equally determined to award the hero the full credit for his heroism. Carlyle vehemently denied that the great man, or any man, acquires power from sources outside his will. In the first *Heroes* lecture he mocked those "critics" who, when shown a great man, "begin to what they call 'account' for him; not to worship him, but take the dimension of him." They make the hero a mere product of circumstances and conditions; they say that "the Time called him forth, the Time did everything, he nothing—but what we the little critic could have done too!" (CW 5:12). The outside forces to which Emerson attributed human greatness are of course far loftier than the mechanical explanations ridiculed in Carlyle's diatribe, but a crucial distinction separates the two writers. Carlyle sought to preserve the great man's free will. Emerson gave all the credit to forces beyond human volition.

In actual practice, the distinction was not always discernible in the events of a subject's life or in the interpretation the biographer brought to those events. Neither man would superimpose theories onto realities. Emerson was quick to praise an act of courage; he could speak without hesitation of Martin Luther's "indomitable Will" in standing alone against the world. In "The Hero as Prophet," Carlyle solemnly defined the essence of Islam (and Christianity as well) as both "Denial of Self" and unquestioning submission to God or "Necessity," and in "The Hero as Poet" he described the great man as a "Force of Nature" (CW 5:56-57, 112). Carlyle and Emerson chose their language with care, but they felt no compulsion to use even their most significant terms with rigorous consistency from one work to the next. In the final analysis, the true differences between them are best seen in their art, not in their philosophy, for it was in the actual process of narration, in a biographical piece, that each man revealed the true nature of his convictions. The biographical methods they used reflected their beliefs more than the particular life stories they chose to record.

Carlyle always strove for identification with his subject, and the greater his sympathy, the more completely he tried to merge himself with his hero. Emerson maintained his detachment even when his passions were most aroused. His restraint can be observed in an early lecture on Luther, the best in the "Biography" series of 1835. Three years earlier, he had thought of Luther when he resigned from the Second Church; after preaching his farewell sermon he copied in his journal a paraphrase of Luther's defiant speech to the Diet of Worms.[18] (Unknown to him at the time, the unsigned article in *Fraser's Magazine* from which he drew the quotation was by Carlyle.) As he prepared his talk on Luther, he must have relived the day when he had nailed theses of his own to the church door, but a listener ignorant of Emerson's own history would scarcely suspect the extent of his emotional involvement with his subject:

> He deemed himself the conspicuous object of hatred to Satan and his kingdom, and to be sustained against their malice by special interpositions of God. This is the secret of his indomitable Will. No man in history ever assumed a more commanding attitude or expressed a more perfect self-reliance. His words are more than brave, they threaten and thunder. They indicate a Will on which a nation might lean, not liable to sullen sallies or swoons, but progressive as the motion of the earth.[19]

With an almost scientific objectivity, he identified the sources of Luther's courage and the reasons for his ultimate victory. Luther's "perfect self-reliance" came from his trust in an external power which can raise nations and topple kingdoms. The perils Emerson faced in his battle of conscience were a little less awesome than the temporal and supernatural potentates confronting Luther, but in his isolation the young American preacher may have felt as great a need for sustenance as the young German monk. The spiritual bond he felt with Luther can be seen in his quiet fervor.

Carlyle was also attracted to Luther. In 1830 he contemplated a full-length biography of him, though little came of it. In 1839 John Sterling's adulatory review article on Carlyle, which pleased its subject immensely, ended by comparing him with Luther.[20] But he had not undergone a personal experience comparable to the crisis which led Emerson to draw consolation and strength from Luther's example; yet in "The Hero as Priest" his identification with Luther amounted to a virtual metamorphosis. At one point, without warning, the pronouns change their antecedents:

> I, for one, pardon Luther for now altogether revolting against the Pope. The elegant Pagan, by this fire-decree of his, had kindled into noble just wrath the bravest heart then living in this world. The bravest, if also one of the humblest, peaceablest; it was now kindled. These words of mine, words of truth and soberness, aiming faithfully, as human inability would allow, to promote God's truth on Earth, and save men's souls, you, God's vicegerent on earth, answer them by the hangman and fire? You will burn me and them, for answer to the God's-message they strove to bring you? *You* are not God's vicegerent; you are another's than his, I think! I take your Bull, as an emparchmented Lie, and burn *it*. You will do what you see good next: this is what I do. (CW 5:133)

Carlyle was an animated lecturer, especially when excited, and the audience must have found it rather unsettling to see the speaker, abruptly transformed into a fire-breathing Luther, upbraiding his listeners as though they had been transformed into the scarlet woman.

Emerson described how Luther's words "threaten and thunder"; Carlyle threatened and thundered. Emerson's Luther was sustained against his enemies; Carlyle's Luther took the Papal Bull and burned it. Emerson stood outside his subject, even when his sympathy was greatest, and tried to account for the universal truth on which his great man's power relied. Carlyle stepped inside his subject to demonstrate the hero's triumph over limitation. One insisted on objectivity; the other demanded intense emotional commitment.

Carlyle and Emerson were biographers all their lives. Although Emerson never attempted a full-length biography of a single figure, he wrote and lectured about individual men and women — historical and comtemporary, famous and obscure — throughout his career. His last public reading was probably the talk on Carlyle he delivered in February 1881, a few days after Carlyle's death and little more than a year before his own.[21] Carlyle's decline, literary as well as physical, was hastened by his mammoth biography of Frederick the Great. In the remainder of this discussion I will examine, first of all, their approach to two historical figures regarded by both writers as the preeminent men of their age; then, to observe the biographical process on a more personal level, I will take up briefly each man's elegiac response to a young friend who died tragically.

"Of great men," Carlyle once wrote in a review piece, "among so many millions of noted men, it is computed that in our time there have been Two; one in the practical, another in the speculative province: Napoleon Buonaparte and Johann Wolfgang von Goethe" (CW 27:398). In *Representative Men* Emerson set the same two apart in a similar manner. Before he met Carlyle he had called Napoleon "the great Hand of our age" for his engineering and road building, and eventually he came to agree with Carlyle that Goethe was "the pivotal man of the old and new times."[22] Like every other inhabitant of the Western hemisphere in the middle part of the nineteenth century, they were both acquainted with Napoleon's name since childhood. Much of Emerson's knowledge of Goethe was acquired from Carlyle, whose first success in life had come as the translator and advocate of Goethe and other German writers for English-speaking readers. Before he ever heard his name, it will be recalled, Emerson knew Carlyle as his "Germanick new-light writer."

A sharp dispute concerning Goethe runs through some of their early correspondence. In his second letter Emerson consoled Carlyle for the failure of *Sartor Resartus* to find a large audience by strangely suggesting that Carlyle's obscurity somehow proved his moral superiority to Goethe:

> Far far better seems to me the unpopularity of this Philosophical Poem . . . than the adulation that followed your eminent friend Goethe. With him I am becoming better acquainted, but mine must be a qualified admiration. It is a singular piece of good nature in you to apotheosize him. I cannot but regard it as his misfortune with conspicuous bad influence on his genius, — that velvet life he led. What incongruity for genius whose fit ornaments & reliefs are poverty & hatred, to repose fifty years in chairs of state; & what pity that his Duke did not cut off his head to save him from the mean end (forgive) of retiring from the municipal incense "to arrange tastefully his gifts & medals." Then the Puritan in me accepts no apology for bad morals in such as *he*. (L, p. 107)

Even without the anal jest ("forgive") about decapitation and the sarcastic remark on apotheosis, Emerson's attack on Goethe must have touched Carlyle in a sensitive spot. But apparently he was more disturbed by Emerson's *soi-disant* Puritanism; in his reply, as I mentioned before, he reasserted his own Calvinist credentials: "It is impossible you can be more of a Puritan than I" (p. 114). (Earlier in the same letter he reminded Emerson of his own much less remote Unitarian background by left-handedly complimenting him as "the only man I ever met with of that persuasion whom I could unobstructedly like.") He defended Goethe calmly and even partly agreed with Emerson regarding what he

called "Goethe the Heathen"; "But you will know Goethe
the Christian by and by," he insisted, "and like that one far
better" (p. 115). The miniature controversy pretty much
subsided after Emerson's next letter. "The good people
think he overpraises Goethe," he wrote, after describing the
efforts of Carlyle's American friends to publicize *Sartor.*
"There I give him up to their wrath" (p. 120).

Carlyle's forebearance is largely attributable to his affection for Emerson, but it is also true that his hero worship of
Goethe was not quite so pure as he wanted his review readers
to think. The Carlyle-Goethe correspondence provides an
instructive contrast with the Carlyle-Emerson correspondence especially with regard to differences in tone. As we
have seen, he attempted from time to time to commission
Emerson as his American lieutenant, efforts resisted by
Emerson through various means ranging from subterfuge to
nearly outright defiance, but on the whole their epistolary
relationship remained an animated dialogue between
equals. But with Goethe, understandably to be sure, he
made his perfect self-abasement clear from the outset of
their correspondence, never varying the tone of the declaration in his second letter that "It is you more than any other
man that I should always thank and reverence with the feeling of a Disciple to his Master, nay of a Son to his spiritual
Father." For his part, Goethe frequently expressed his ap-
preciation of Carlyle's work on behalf of German literature
in England and encouraged him to go further, but he accepted his pious humility at face value and addressed him
with appropriate paternalism. His blunt directive to him to
keep his distance from the Saint-Simonians is typical of
Goethe's manner. Similarly, in answer to a disparagement
of Utilitarianism, he reminded Carlyle that much of his own
work was "capable of practical application. If you will
admit that there may be idealist Utilitarians also," he
added, a trifle haughtily, "I should be very glad to be
allowed to reckon myself as one of them." It is difficult to
imagine Carlyle keeping his composure while reading about

idealist Utilitarians. In his edition of the Carlyle-Goethe correspondence, Charles Eliot Norton wisely included a letter Carlyle sent in 1828 to his brother John, who was then in Germany studying medicine, asking him to travel to Weimar and see whether Goethe was getting senile, "for daily he grows more inexplicable to me. One letter is written like an oracle, the next shall be too redolent of *twaddle*."[23] What Emerson called his apotheosis of Goethe clearly did not affect his objectivity, at least in private, about Goethe the person, as opposed to Goethe the poet. Much of his difficulty with Goethe is attributable to his inability or unwillingness to separate the man from the hero.

His admiration for Goethe the poet was heartfelt. In his first letter to Goethe, which accompanied a copy of his translation of *Wilhelm Meister's Apprenticeship,* he took the opportunity to acknowledge a personal debt to the author of *Faust.* "Four years ago," he wrote, "when I read your *Faust* among the mountains of my native Scotland, I could not but fancy I might one day see you, and pour out before you, as before a Father, the woes and wanderings of a heart whose mysteries you seemed so thoroughly to comprehend, and could so beautifully represent."[24] Four years earlier, in 1820, Carlyle had been at the nadir of his miserable young manhood, of what in 1825 he called his "long dismal seven years of pain."[25] The positive events of his youth, the Leith Walk and Hoddam Hill "conversions," the beginnings of literary recognition, and his marriage, were all in the future. Reading *Faust* meant much to him.

All readers of *Sartor Resartus* are aware of the prominence accorded *Faust* and Goethe generally as Carlyle's inspiration. But the true significance of *Faust* in the development of his mind is best seen in an essay he wrote in 1828, wherein he described Goethe's hero as "the son of Light and Free-will" who joins with evil in a noble but hopeless battle against fate, hopeless because he channels his energy in the wrong direction. According to Carlyle, Faust suffers from "Pride, and an entire uncompromising though secret love of Self"; in fact, his condition is similar to that in which Teufelsdröckh's shoeblack would find himself a few years later:

> Go where he may, he will "find himself again in a conditional world"; widen his sphere as he pleases, he will find it again encircled by the empire of Necessity; the gay island of Existence is again but a fraction of the ancient realm of Night . . . The poorest human soul is infinite in wishes, and the infinite Universe was not made for one, but for all. Vain were it for Faust, by heaping height on height, to struggle towards infinitude; while to that law of Self-Denial, by which alone man's narrow destiny may become an infinitude within itself, he is still a stranger. (CW 26:160-161)

He discovered in *Faust* an expression of his own solution to the problem of existence: self-denial as a means of resolving in favor of freedom the conflict between freedom and fate. "Everywhere the human soul stands between a hemisphere of light and another of darkness," he wrote in another essay on Goethe, "on the confines of two everlastingly hostile empires, Necessity and Freewill" (CW 27:405). Goethe's triumph in this clash of empires became an article of faith to him because he had committed his own hopes for victory and freedom to his interpretation of Goethe's life and work. Reading Goethe's "inward life" through his writings, he explained in "Goethe's Works" (1832), "We see this above all things: A mind working itself into clearer and clearer freedom; gaining a more and more perfect dominion of its world" (p. 430).

The intensity of his commitment accounts for his obstinate defense of Goethe's morality, which he accomplished through such techniques as proposing "Pagan" and "Christian" phases (as in the letter to Emerson), simple mitigation of lapses Goethe himself confessed in his autobiography, disingenuous attempts at sheer mystification, and satiric derision of the "circulating-library" morals of Goethe's detractors (cf. CW 27:419-422, 431-435). Probably his most

significant defense of Goethe, and certainly the most revealing psychologically, was his apparently unconscious revision
of a line of Goethe's poetry. His brief death notice for
Goethe ends with a magisterial injunction to his readers to
"live, as he counselled and commanded, not commodiously
in the Reputable, the Plausible, the Half, but resolutely in
the Whole, the Good, the True: '*Im Ganzen, Guten,
Wahren resolut zu leben!*' " (CW 27:384). In both the English and the German Carlyle substitutes "true" (*Wahren*) for
Goethe's "beautiful" (*Schönen*). The substitution, which of
course radically alters the meaning, cannot be deliberate,
for he had once made the same mistake writing to Goethe
himself.[26] The simple replacement of one word by another,
trivial in itself, reveals much about his attitude toward Goethe; it may also foreshadow a profound change in Carlyle's
life.

His loss of interest in purely literary subjects after 1840 is
demonstrable from a chronology of his works. The turn
away from literature resembles his abandonment of religious
speculation after *Sartor Resartus,* and a common approach
to the study of Carlyle combines the two reactions and explains them as the conquest of his "transcendentalism" or
"romanticism" by his "puritanism."[27] I have argued that his
projected resurrection of Christian immortality, supposedly
on the basis of German metaphysics, finally collapsed when
confronted with the inescapability of death. He reached this
point (whether or not he himself realized it) while writing
"Natural Supernaturalism"; afterwards he in effect gave up
on religion in general. He had also undertaken a related
philosophical project centered upon the freedom of the self,
freedom which is not dependent on God. This project never
collapsed entirely, but it was greatly weakened, I believe, by
his immense emotional investment in one man, Goethe. He
hardly thought of Kant, Fichte, and the rest of his German
philosophers as more than sources of ideas, actually as
sources of terms on which to hang his own ideas, as on pegs.
He virtually replaced them all with the whimsical buffoon

Teufelsdröckh just as soon as he realized the literary advantages of doing so. He also dressed Goethe in his own ideas, but emotionally he went much further. Emotionally, he placed on Goethe the greater part, the ideal part, of himself. No one man, however great a hero, could bear such a burden. Goethe could no more embody Carlyle's ideal self than Carlyle could permanently lose himself in an idealized Goethe. Keats's urn to the contrary, truth and beauty are not necessarily the same; sooner or later he would come to suspect that he and Goethe might not necessarily choose between truth and beauty in the same way.

Now is the time to introduce some "evidence," but unfortunately the only evidence I have to offer is not in anything Carlyle wrote but rather in what he failed to write. He failed, first of all, to write a full-scale biography of Goethe, although he had entertained proposals for one as early as 1830.[28] It is true that Goethe had written an autobiography, but Carlyle, with his broad reading and literary sophistication, surely would have agreed with A. O. J. Cockshut that the "difference between biography and autobiography is fundamental; and it is seen in its chemically pure state when each is true and good in its own way and when most of the working materials are the same."[29] It is also true that he did write several review articles on Goethe, two of which, "Goethe" (1828) and "Goethe's Works" (1832), are of substantial length. These pieces, however, are works of advocacy rather than of interpretation; he still considered himself Goethe's proponent in England rather than his critic and biographer. Most puzzling is his failure to include in *Heroes and Hero-Worship* the man who in so many ways had been his greatest hero and his most personal hero as well. The manner in which he explained the incongruity helps only slightly to solve the puzzle. For one thing, he announced the omission of Goethe in "The Hero as Man of Letters" rather than in "The Hero as Poet," so that while dismissing Goethe he was also demoting him to a lower order. And his haste is significant; he gave Goethe less than two paragraphs. "Our chosen specimen of the Hero as Literary Man would be this Goethe," he admitted in the first paragraph, after some empty words about Goethe's Fichtean "vision of the inward divine mystery." He assured himself that "it were a very pleasant plan for me here to discourse of his heroism: for I consider him to be a true Hero; heroic in what he said and did, and perhaps still more in what he did not say and did not do; to me a noble spectacle: a great heroic ancient man, speaking and keeping silence as an ancient Hero, in the guise of a most modern, high-bred, high-cultivated Man of Letters!" Perhaps in that last part about the "guise" of high breeding and cultivation there is a faint trace of disillusionment and regret. Certainly there is little amidst the platitudes to recall the "mind working itself into clearer and clearer freedom" of eight years earlier. In the next paragraph he dropped Goethe abruptly, and, as it turned out, forever. The "general state of knowledge about Goethe," he explained, makes speaking about him "worse than useless." "Speak as I might, Goethe, to the great majority of you, would remain problematic, vague; no impression but a false one could be realised. Him we must leave to future times," and he rushed off in mid-sentence to Johnson, Burns, and Rousseau (CW 5:157-158). He may have felt that he would leave a false impression even if he spoke the truth.[30]

Unfulfilled hero worship of Goethe may have hastened the near destruction of Carlyle's project of freedom, but it was surely inevitable that his championship of free will eventually would fall victim to eternal necessity, just as his hope for immortality collapsed before the plain fact of death. Like the phoenix cycles in his own theory of history, Carlyle's intellectual development followed a pattern of fervid affirmation ending in hopeless disintegration. When he insisted on pressing his thoughts and passions to an extremity, contradictions would arise that he could not resolve and would not accept. So he would give up the struggle, withdraw into silence on the matter, and take up something more promising. The cooler Emerson, on the other hand, armed with a constitutional capacity for emotional detachment, had nothing to fear from contradictions, inconsistencies, and other hobgoblins of little minds. He knew when to pull back before the contradictions overwhelmed him. And his fatalism was broad enough to encompass seemingly antithetical tendencies, even freedom itself, or at least the nonconformist's freedom in "Self-Reliance"—the very kind of freedom, in fact, that he accused Goethe of lacking.

Emerson's first substantial public statement on Goethe appeared in "Thoughts on Modern Literature" (1840). He probably came to regret the harshness of his language in that article ("vicious subjectiveness," "total want of frankness") five years later when he prepared the far superior lecture on Goethe for *Representative Men,* but there is a remarkable moment in the earlier piece where he seems to measure Goethe and find him wanting by Carlyle's own standards. Goethe is denounced as "the poet of the Actual, not of the Ideal; the poet of limitation, not of possibility; of this world, and not of religion and hope; . . . the poet of prose, and not of poetry." Furthermore, Goethe "accepts the base doctrine of Fate, and gleans what straggling joys may yet remain out of its ban"; he "dares not break from his slavery and lead a man's life in a man's relation to Nature." Carlyle, who read the essay in *The Dial,* must have been startled by the part about fate and by Emerson's charge that Goethe never sought to "abolish the old heavens and the old earth before the free will or Godhead of man" (EW 12:331).

Emerson's animus against Goethe, here and in general, was largely the product, oddly enough, of an old family grudge. In 1824 his older brother William, then a student at Göttingen, went to Weimar to consult Goethe on questions of conscience troubling him as a result of his exposure to German biblical criticism. The purport of Goethe's advice was not to let theological scruples stand in the way of a successful career in the ministry.[31] Faced with a similar dilemma twelve years later, it will be recalled, Emerson turned for help to the "indomitable Will" and "perfect self-reliance" of Martin Luther. And so when he rails against Goethe's submission to "the base doctrine of Fate," he is really talking about, or at least thinking about, accommodation to society.

The application of terms like "fate" and "free will" to Goethe may have been calculated to renew the Goethe debate with Carlyle. But if any provocation was intended, Carlyle refused the challenge. He had nothing but praise for Emerson's paper, which was "incomparably the worthiest thing hitherto" in *The Dial* (although it was only the second number). "Even what you say of Goethe gratifies me," he declared; "it is one of the few things yet spoken of him from personal insight." He cleverly neutralized Emerson's charge that Goethe was "actual" rather than "ideal" by suggesting that in a sense they are both the same; perhaps he had in mind Goethe the "idealist Utilitarian" of years ago. In any case, he was confident that "one day" Emerson would understand "that this sunny-looking, courtly Goethe held veiled in him a Prophetic sorrow"—a sorrow which, he added rather strangely, was "all the nobler" because "he could not so hold it" (L, p. 287). Perhaps Carlyle, who had finished writing out the *Heroes* lectures for publication a few months earlier, read into Emerson's "personal insight" (just how personal Carlyle probably never knew) some personal insights of his own that he had failed to speak. But the rest of his comments in the letter resemble the curt farewell to Goethe in "The Hero as Man of Letters," pious but pointless.

In *Representative Men* Emerson reversed some of his criticisms of Goethe, modified others, and heightened his recognition of Goethe's achievements (in contrast to the earlier tone of grudging admiration). He again seemed to have Carlyle in back of his thoughts, although Carlyle is never mentioned. He followed Carlyle in classifying Goethe as "The Writer" rather than "The Poet," but the impact is blunted by the plan of *Representative Men,* which permits only one subject per essay (Shakespeare of course is "The

Poet"). He did not deny Goethe the name of poet or call him "the poet of prose and not of poetry" as in the *Dial* article, though he confined his analysis of Goethe's writings almost exclusively to prose works, particularly *Wilhelm Meister*. He barely alluded to *Faust*. But on the whole his presentation of Goethe was affirmative; after all, Goethe was his last representative man.

Carlyle's presence may be felt in other, more subtle ways; for example, in contrast to the fatalistic Goethe of the *Dial* piece, Emerson now perceived in him "a heart-cheering freedom in his speculation." At the same time, he also found admirable Emersonian qualities, particularly with regard to Goethe's interest in natural science: he "has said the best things about nature that ever were said" (EW 4:273-276). For Emerson, there was no higher praise. Again he applied Carlyle's criteria to Goethe, but this time he allowed Goethe unlimited aspirations for "the conquest of universal nature" and "universal truth," the integrity "not to be bribed, nor deceived, nor overawed," and "a stoical self-command and self-denial." Yet his primary reservation about Goethe persisted, only now the terms of condemnation were more recognizably his own. "He has not worshipped the highest unity; he is incapable of a self-surrender to the moral sentiment." In other words, Goethe was lacking in self-reliance; indeed, he had rejected self-reliance and pursued in its place self-cultivation. "There are writers poorer in talent, whose tone is purer, and more touches the heart. Goethe can never be dear to men. His is not even the devotion to pure truth; but to truth for the sake of culture" (p. 284). Emerson was not about to repeat Carlyle's error and substitute his own truth for Goethe's beauty.

By the end of the essay, Goethe's "calculations of self-culture" merge with Emerson's more personal charge against him, accommodation to the expectations of society. Goethe "was entirely at home and happy in his century and the world. None was so fit to live, or more heartily enjoyed the game." Goethe's pleasure in the world agrees with the "aim of culture, which is the genius of his works." But for Emerson the "idea of absolute, eternal truth, without reference to my own enlargement by it is higher" (pp. 288-289).

Typically, Emerson reserved the severest criticisms for the conclusion of each section. The systematic objectivity of *Representative Men,* perhaps its outstanding quality, can be attributed to his dialectical approach to his subjects, which counters praise with detraction and in the end tries to "strike the balance" (as he put it in the chapter on Shakespeare). Perhaps he felt compelled to adopt so rigid a method in order to restrain his own impulse to identify with his heroes, and in this regard it may be significant that he omitted Luther entirely. His procedure assured detachment and reinforced the message in the introduction that great men should be "used" and not worshipped, but it also demanded that he cut his subjects down to size.

Writing to Emerson in 1850, shortly after the simultaneous English and American publication of the book, Carlyle offered his congratulations and hopes for its immediate success and praised the quality of the "portraitures." He "generally dissented," however, "a little about the *end* of all those Essays; which was notable, and not without instructive interest to me, as I had so lustily shouted 'Hear, hear!' all the way from the beginning up to that stage" (L, p. 460). Since Emerson usually concentrated his negative judgments "a little about the end," we can guess the source of Carlyle's annoyance. It was not just a matter of undermining great men; Carlyle would have agreed that some "great men" deserved to be undermined. But he knew that most of the tarnished subjects of *Representative Men* were figures whom Emerson greatly admired. He told Emerson in the letter that he liked the Plato section the least. Carlyle was never fond of Plato, so one might think that he would be pleased to see Platonism dismissed as "a thing of shreds and patches" (EW 4:77). But he knew that Plato was one of Emerson's favorite thinkers; yet here and throughout the book Emerson insisted on disparaging his own heroes. Swedenborg's work was a rotting corpse complete with "charnel-breath" (p. 144); Montaigne the skeptic became an amoral cynic, "content with just and unjust, with sots and fools, with the triumph of folly and fraud" (p. 183); and Shakespeare, a "Priest of Mankind" to Carlyle in "The Hero as Poet," was accused by Emerson of leading "an obscure and profane life, using his genius for the public amusement" (p. 218). Carlyle would have expected some criticism of Goethe and may actually have been surprised by the generosity of Emerson's assessment. But why must he deliberately reduce the stature of the great men most dear to him? Carlyle could only wonder, for his methods were quite different from the cool dialectics of Emerson.

In *Heroes and Hero-Worship* Carlyle successively parades his heroes according to his own biographical formula: a hero is named; Carlyle's passions are ignited and he *becomes* the hero; the flame dies and he moves on to ignite another. As with Emerson, the pattern of exposition reflects his beliefs. His utter rejection of the idea that "the Times" produce the hero inspires in the first lecture an image of the times as "dry dead fuel, waiting for the lightning out of Heaven that shall kindle it. The great man, with his free force direct out of God's own hand, is the lightning" (CW 5:13). He is trying to have it both ways with the "free force direct out of God's own hand" (how could it then be free?), but the point is that the lightning, and not the "dry mouldering sticks," creates the fire. To capture the power of the hero, the hero worshipper must overcome his own deadness and burst into sympathetic flame. And in lecture after lecture, hero after hero, the lightning strikes Carlyle on schedule and he promptly flares up in enthusiastic identification until the flames subside. He was too good a craftsman to kill an image by working it to death, however, so he uses the actual lightning and fire sparingly. The obvious application to the Norse gods in "The Hero as Divinity" is repeated in "The Hero as Priest" where the child Martin Luther is described as "a Christian Odin,—a right Thor once more, with his thunder-hammer, to smite asunder ugly enough *Jötuns* and Giant-monsters" (p. 128). (Somewhat incongruously, in the very next paragraph young Martin's playmate Alexis is struck dead "by lightning, at the gate of Erfurt.") Similarly, the age of "Mahomet" in "The Hero as Prophet" was "as if a spark had fallen, one spark, on a world of what seemed black unnoticeable sand; but lo, the sand proves explosive powder, blazes heaven-high from Delhi to Grenada!" (p. 77). And of Rousseau, with whom he had little sympathy, he writes, "There is no good in emitting *smoke* till you have made it into *fire,* —which, in the metaphorical sense too, all smoke is capable of becoming" (p. 184). Apparently Rousseau fizzled out because of wet sticks or feeble lightning bolts.

At the end of *Heroes and Hero-Worship,* when he comes to Napoleon, "our last Great Man," the lightning image itself sputters out, or what is worse, becomes a sort of ignis fatuus:

> Napoleon's working, accordingly, what was it with all the noise it made? A flash as of gunpowder wide-spread; a blazing-up as of dry heath. For an hour the whole Universe seems wrapt in smoke and flame: but only for an hour. It goes out: the Universe with its old mountains and streams, its stars above and kind soil beneath, is still there. (p. 242)

Instead of attaining eternal greatness through self-denial, Napoleon betrayed his own heroism through "untruth of heart," or just plain egoism. "*Self* and false ambition had now become his god: *self*-deception once yielded to, *all* other deceptions follow naturally." Hence his proverbially false bulletins. Furthermore, instead of ennobling his followers through true hero worship, he used them for his own selfish ends: "he believed too much in the *Dupeability* of men; saw no fact deeper in man than Hunger and this!" Because of his failure to embody in himself and inspire in others the qualities of self-denial, he lost everything. "Like a

man that should build upon cloud; his house and he fall
down in confused wreck, and depart out of the world" (p.
241).

Compared with Carlyle's ideal ruler, Oliver Cromwell,
Napoleon was really a little man; he does not forbear ridi-
culing the physical shortness of his hero *manqué*. Napoleon's hemispheric conquests, though much greater than the
insular victories of Cromwell, nonetheless "are but as the
high *stilts* on which the man is seen standing; the stature of
the man is not altered thereby" (p. 237). In keeping with his
Germanophilism, the "palpable tyrannous murderous injustice" for which he judges Napoleon rightly doomed is the
execution of "that poor German Bookseller, Palm," rather
than the crime which weighs more heavily in other British
treatments of Napoleon (such as those of Scott and Hazlitt),
the killing of the Duc d'Enghien. What surprises most in
Carlyle's brief glance at Napoleon is its objectivity, its almost Emersonian detachment. He allows Napoleon his virtues, mainly his fidelity to the reforming spirit of the French
Revolution, and he condemns his faults without exorbitant
denunciation. Even his language takes on an Emersonian
coolness. "What Napoleon *did* will in the long-run amount
to what he did *justly*; what Nature with her laws will sanc-
tion. To what of reality was in him; to that and nothing
more. The rest was all smoke and waste" (p. 242). Only in
the pity and sadness with which the lecture concludes does
something of Carlyle's emotional intensity survive. Napoleon "had gone that way of his; and Nature also had gone
her way. Having once parted with Reality, he tumbles helpless in Vacuity; no rescue for him. He had to sink there,
mournfully as man seldom did; and break his great heart,
and die" (p. 243). Napoleon seems more real than Carlyle's
other heroes because Carlyle recognizes how much of him
was false. For once, the thundering big man becomes a little
man on stilts.

Carlyle must have been pleased with Emerson's "Napoleon, or, The Man of the World," which represents essen-

tially the same stilt-walker, although Emerson found more to admire. The phrase "man of the world" suggests both sides of his dialectic: the irresistible world conqueror and the ambitious upstart who knew how to get ahead. Emerson's Napoleon was well in tune with his fate, at least at first. "He respected the power of nature and fortune, and ascribed to it his superiority, instead of valuing himself, like inferior men, on his opinionativeness, and waging war with nature." In other words, Napoleon agreed with Emerson about the source of his greatness; "He pleased himself, as well as the people, when he styled himself the 'Child of Destiny' " (EW 4:231). Like Carlyle, Emerson admired Napoleon's anti-aristocratic spirit, though he stressed the bourgeois and democratic aspects of Napoleon's reforms to a greater degree than would have pleased Carlyle. And whereas Carlyle had simply ignored the Duc d'Enghien affair, and one of Emerson's mentors, William Ellery Channing, had condemned the murder in terms as strong as Walter Scott's, Emerson approvingly repeated Napoleon's own answer to the charge of spilling noble blood: "Neither is my blood ditchwater" (p. 242).

The Napoleon piece may have been the only chapter in *Representative Men* whose ending Carlyle could genuinely approve; except for the first sentence, Emerson's conclusions about Napoleon's downfall were in accord with his own:

> It was not Bonaparte's fault. He did all that in him lay to live and thrive without moral principle. It was the nature of things, the eternal law of man and of the world which baulked and ruined him . . . Every experiment, by multitudes or by individuals, that has a sensual and selfish aim, will fail. (p. 258)

Carlyle would not have agreed that it was not Bonaparte's fault, and he might have accused Emerson of being unfair to Napoleon and of lacking compassion, even for the murderer of Palm the bookseller. When all responsibility is placed on nature and destiny, the criminal is exonerated,

but he is robbed of the pity which the guilty may sometimes
extract from the innocent.

For all the talk of sincerity in *Heroes and Hero-Worship,*
Carlyle's technique of total identification with his subjects
sometimes creates an undesirably theatrical, if not fraudu-
lent, impression. The passage from "The Hero as Priest"
where he metamorphoses into an indignant Luther is a good
example of the strengths and weaknesses of his methods.
The device is effective to the extent that we are able to forget about the historical Luther and accept the speaker for
what he unquestionably remains: Carlyle himself as a
modern-day Luther indignantly burning the Papal Bulls of
another era. Only those would object who actually wanted
to hear Carlyle speak about Luther rather than just to hear
Carlyle. (The *Heroes* book is best appreciated today when
the reader imagines it being delivered in its original form, as
lectures.) His biographical writings may succeed as literary
productions by Thomas Carlyle, but they often fail as the
representations of other people. "We are left half-con-
vinced," wrote A. O. J. Cockshut recently of a danger endemic to the entire genre, "that the man really was the man
the biographer saw"; but with Carlyle this problem is largely
irrelevant, since the man the biographer saw was usually
himself.[32] And the irony is that Carlyle turned to biography
in the first place to escape the shadow of himself through
hero worship of someone greater.

Because for once his subject was not someone greater, to
be worshipped as a hero, but a friend and equal, to be loved
as a brother, Carlyle's *Life of John Sterling* (1851) is his most
successful life study, one of his best books of any kind, and a
minor masterpiece of Victorian biography.[33] In writing
Sterling's life, he reversed his usual procedure; instead of
creating a hero for ordinary people to emulate, he presented
an interesting but not extraordinary man whose "Pilgrimage
through our poor Nineteenth Century" should serve to
remind the great and all who would be great of their

common humanity with everyone else. "I have remarked," he wrote in the first chapter, recalling a passage in his old essay on "Biography," "that a true delineation of the smallest man, and his scene of pilgrimage through life, is capable of interesting the greatest man"; and he added that "each man's life" is "a strange emblem of every man's" (CW 11:7).

Along with Tennyson's friend Hallam and Hurrell Froude, the older brother of Carlyle's own biographer, John Sterling belonged to a class prominent in nineteenth-century England: talented men who died young, leaving behind them little more than unfulfilled promise. Carlyle felt so drawn to Sterling, who was eleven years his junior, because few people understood him so well and also because, as he practically admitted, few of his other friends would so readily stand up to him in private conversation, oppose his obstinate harangues, and tell him when he was wrong. Sterling was never his disciple or his hero worshipper. Carlyle was "secretly" so grateful for Sterling's favorable *Westminster Review* piece on him because "for me Sterling, often enough the stiff gainsayer in our private communings, was the doer of this." Perhaps he saw reflected in Sterling his own capacity for "holding out his last position as doggedly as the first: and to some of my notions he seemed to grow in stubbornness of opposition, with the growing inevitability, and never would surrender" (p. 192). But the essence of the book is not Carlyle's personal identification with Sterling. The assumption of such an identification may account for the common misreading of the best-known chapter, the devastating satire on Coleridge, as a repudiation by Carlyle of his own youthful Transcendentalism. But his aim was to reveal a typical life in which the reader can see something of himself, and not, as in a *Heroes* lecture, to impersonate a superhuman marvel and lose himself in lightning-struck awe. In this book there is restrained emotion but no lightning and fire (although at one point there is a hurricane).

Sterling led a varied life, and Carlyle emphasized the variety in order to establish the universality of Sterling's experiences. And although he drew on his own recollections of Coleridge in depicting Sterling's visits to Highgate, the episode probably has no more autobiographical significance than any other event in the narrative. He recounted Sterling's involvement in a desperate conspiracy of Spanish exiles, his unsuccessful management of a plantation in the West Indies, his attenuated career in the ministry, and his failure as a poet, along with the Coleridge encounters (and even the Carlyle encounters) as illustrative of the difficulties faced by an honest man trying to live a decent life in "as mad a world as you could wish." The variety of Sterling's life also supported Carlyle's poetic explanation for its brevity, that "it was the very excess of *life* in him that brought on disease" (p. 123). For Sterling, character was fate.

Emerson also had a friend whose death seemed to him a consequence of her excess of life, though Margaret Fuller died in a shipwreck rather than from consumption. Emerson differentiated Fuller from himself by contrasting their respective temperaments:

> When I found she lived at a rate so much faster than mine, and which was violent compared with mine, I foreboded rash and painful crises, and had a feeling as if a voice cried, *Stand from under!*— as if, a little further on, this destiny was threatened with jars and reverses, which no friendship could avert or console. This feeling partly wore off, on better acquaintance, but remained latent; and I had always an impression that her energy was too much a force of blood, and therefore never felt the security for her peace which belongs to more purely intellectual natures. She seemed more vulnerable. For the same reason, she remained inscrutable to me; her strength was not my strength, —her powers were a surprise.[34]

Character was destiny for Fuller, too, which accorded not only with Emerson's philosophy but with Fuller's own "faith more or less distinct in a fate, and in a guardian genius" (p. 219). Notwithstanding her "inscrutability," Emerson's Fuller sometimes seems to embody tendencies present in

Emerson himself, but which he insisted on keeping in check. She was an emotional Emerson, an Emerson without detachment, an Emerson who lived at a faster rate and had a greater "force of blood." She had "a certain pathos of sentiment, and a march of character, threatening to arrive presently at the shores and plunge into the sea of Buddhism and mystical trances." Emerson himself was, of course, very interested in Eastern religions and in mysticism, but he never experienced the "ecstasy" claimed by Fuller. He refused to accept her description of her new "frame of mind" as "profound or permanent," and he ascribed her anger at his "want of sympathy" to "a certain restlessness and fever, which I did not like should deceive a soul which was capable of greatness" (pp. 308-309). The relationship between the two, in short, was as dynamic in its way as the friendship of Carlyle and Sterling. Fuller stood as an equal before Emerson. At one point he recalls "congratulating myself on the solid good understanding that subsisted between us," only to be "surprised with hearing it taxed by her with superficiality and halfness" (p. 288).

Margaret Fuller did not become a surrogate Emerson, though he brought to his memoir of her a sense of personal involvement rare in his biographical writings on historical figures. Nor did she become a nineteenth-century pilgrim, though at the end he praised her, simply, as "a right brave and heroic woman" (p. 300). Had he attempted an independent, full-scale biography of Margaret Fuller, rather than confining himself to the ten years when he "knew her intimately," he might have produced an Emersonian *Life of Sterling*. Carlyle's book was surely on his mind as he prepared his contribution to the Fuller memorial volumes, not only because of the similarities between Fuller and Sterling but also because Emerson was a friend of both the woman and the man.[35]

Carlyle and Emerson turned to biography from Transcendentalism because they had decided that, as Emerson

put it, the most important questions are best answered in a
life and not in a book; and on the whole they declared their
convictions on freedom and fate, on self-denial and self-
reliance, more forcefully, if not more convincingly, in their
biographical writings than in their speculative essays. The
histories of heroes and representative men, when read for
the philosophical ideas which underlie them, attain a dramatic intensity seldom achieved in strictly philosophical
writing. The philosophy does not overwhelm the biography
because both authors had the simple ability to bring life to
characters in a book, a talent observable in its pure form,
free of didactic strategies, in the lives they wrote of their
friends. They also revealed more of their own personalities
when they wrote about people they actually knew. And they
stand before us most clearly, or so I have found, in the letters they wrote to each other. After all, what is writing of
any kind but self-revelation?

3

Past and Present: England and America

In 1845 a Philadelphia publisher sent Emerson a print of an engraving proposed for the frontispiece to a new edition of Carlyle's *Miscellanies*. "They were eager to have the engraving pronounced a good likeness," Emerson wrote Carlyle, but he could fulfill the request only by showing it to others "who have seen you long since I had." And they all "shook their heads" (L, p. 379). Carlyle was not disturbed by the admission that his best friend in America no longer knew what he looked like. On the contrary, he assured Emerson that in preference to "that frightful picture" (which the Philadelphia firm printed anyway) or "indeed any picture at all, I had rather stand as a shadow than as a falsity" (p. 381). Emerson, too, was satisfied, for although he could no longer envision Carlyle's features, he could always read his letters and books. Soon he would receive the long-awaited volumes on Cromwell. "Why should I regret that I see you not," he wrote, "when you are forced thus intimately to discover yourself beyond the intimacy of conversation" (p. 382). There the matter rested until the following year.

This time it was Carlyle's curiosity about Emerson's appearance that prompted him to send a new daguerreotype to Concord and to demand one from Emerson in return. Even so, he insisted that Emerson's "living face," remembered from thirteen years ago, "remains unchanged within me, enveloped in beautiful clouds, and emerging now and

then into strange clearness!" As it often did, the memory of
Craigenputtock put Carlyle in a sentimental mood: " 'In the
wide Earth,' I say sometimes with a sigh, 'there is none but
Emerson that responds to me with a voice wholly human!' "
(p. 395). In his next letter he expressed the hope that "your
Photograph succeed as well as mine," which was "far beyond
all pictures; really very like." (Jane Carlyle thought it "even
liker"; obviously both were flattered.) Again he grew misty.
"Do you bethink you of Craigenputtock, and the still eve-
ning there? I could burst into tears, if I had that habit; but it
is of no use" (p. 398). Because Carlyle thought for some reason that the exchange of pictures was Emerson's idea, in his
answer Emerson explained that he had *wished* for a picture
of Carlyle but had not asked for one. Then he told Carlyle of
his difficulties in complying with the arrangement. He had
sat for the best daguerreotypist in Boston only to have his
"housemates" declare the results "rueful" and "supremely
ridiculous." One good friend, "true Elizabeth Hoar," advised him to forget the whole thing because he was not "of
the right complexion" for daguerreotyping (p. 398).

He may have been inclined to take that advice until Carlyle's picture arrived. "I have what I have wished," he wrote
back; "I confirm my recollections & I make new observations: it is life to life." The picture is certainly handsome,
the softness of the daguerreotype image harmonizing with
the distant expression on Carlyle's face, which nevertheless
looks strong and vigorous. Emerson was impressed with the
craftsmanship, though he was "accustomed to expect of the
English a securing of the essentials in their work." He felt
"instantly stirred to an emulation of your love & punctual-
ity"; no doubt he also had been affected by the nostalgic
tone of Carlyle's recent letters. And so on his forty-third
birthday he doggedly sat for another daguerreotypist, "who
took much pains to make his picture right" but succeeded as
miserably as his predecessor. "My wife protests against the
imprints as slanderous," he admitted with gentle self-mock-
ery. "My friends say, they look ten years older, and as I

think, with the air of a decayed gentleman touched with his first paralysis." (Years later he wrote in *The Conduct of Life:* "Our bodies do not fit us, but caricature and satirize us.") He decided to send a print to Carlyle anyway, "on the ground that I am not likely to get a better" (p. 400), and with this pose of wounded vanity he meant to put an end to the whole affair.

Carlyle was not satisfied, and the vehemence of his reaction to "this poor shadow" is more than surprising; it is chilling:

> But it must not rest there, no. This Image is altogether un-satisfactory, illusive, and even in some measure tragical to me! First of all, it is a bad Photograph; no eyes discernible, at least one of the eyes not, except in rare favourable lights: then, alas, Time itself and Oblivion must have been busy. I could not at first, nor can I yet with perfect decisiveness, bring out any fea-ture completely recalling to me the old Emerson, that lighted on us from the Blue, at Craigenputtock, long ago, —eheu! Here is a genial, smiling energetic face, full of sunny strength, in-telligence, integrity, good humour; but it lies imprisoned in baleful shades, as of the valley of Death; seems smiling on me as if in mockery, "Dost know me, friend? I am dead, thou seest, and distant, and forever hidden from thee; —I belong already to the Eternities, and thou recognisest me not!" (p. 404)

It would have been out of character for Emerson to take offense at having his personal appearance likened to that of a corpse. However, he did not respond to Carlyle's morbid outburst, nor did he comply with his request for yet another picture. The letter may have brought home a realization of the visionary proportions to which he had grown in Carlyle's mind over the years since Craigenputtock. Carlyle wrote "the old Emerson" but meant the young Emerson, for in Carlyle's memory he remained "unchanged"—still a young man on tour, full of energy and warmth, going out of his way to meet another young man whose talent he had been

among the first to recognize. When Carlyle thought of
Emerson he thought of his own youth, when fame and
security were in the distant future, if anywhere, like old age
and death. The image of the mature Emerson—the con-
striction of the Yankee features exaggerated by the prominence of the parrot-like nose—must have reminded him
that time and oblivion are always busy with everyone,
whether the reflection on the daguerreotypist's plate is
pleasing or not. Carlyle and Emerson were now entering
middle age. Carlyle in particular was anxious in the face of
dissolution and decay; hence his overreaction to Emerson's
picture.

Thus when Emerson began the letter to Carlyle dated 31
July 1847 with "In my old age I am coming to see you," the
words carried a private meaning beyond the simple an-
nouncement of the final arrangements for his second trip to
Europe. As if to add to the poignancy, the letter goes on to
describe some pictures he had obtained of John Sterling,
who had been dead three years. Their youth was past; the
meeting in Chelsea would not recreate the visit to Craigenputtock. Not only were they older, but they knew so much
more about each other. Emerson's letter begs for a hospitable welcome, not entirely in jest:

> I pray you to cherish your good nature, your mercy—let your
> wife cherish it—that I may see, I indolent, this incredible
> worker, whose toil has been long since my pride & wonder, —
> that I may see him benign and unexacting—he shall not be at
> the crisis of some new labor—I shall not stay but an hour—
> what do I care for his fame? (p. 426)

Ascribing to Jane Carlyle, who was her husband's match in
acrimony, the guardianship of his good nature and mercy, is
absurd, but otherwise the assessment of Carlyle's mature
personality implicit in Emerson's plea is remarkably accurate. Carlyle in this period was an "incredible worker" who
was often depressed when he was not working and irritable
when he was. He hated to be disturbed, so Emerson, aware

that his arrival might constitute a disruption whenever it occurred, pledged that his stay would be brief. He knew that Carlyle sometimes thought of him, more than half seriously, as "indolent" and dreamy. On the other hand, he was confident enough of their friendship to reverse his ironically sheepish tone at the end with an abrupt reaffirmation of their equality: "What do I care for his fame?" Emerson, for one, would not allow their mutual celebrity to corrupt a relationship which had begun in mutual obscurity.

Much has been made of the great quarrels Carlyle and Emerson supposedly had when they finally came face to face again after so many years. The most serious clash occurred sometime during Emerson's first week in England, while he was staying with the Carlyles in Chelsea. We have the story second hand from Emerson via George Searle Phillips. A difference of opinion over Cromwell—about what precisely is unknown—ended with Carlyle's "drawing a line with his finger across the table" and saying "with terrible fierceness: Then, sir, there is a line of separation between you and me as wide as that, & as deep as the pit."[1] There is no reason to distrust Phillips; yet his report is the only instance of a verbal conflict serious enough for either man to have lost his temper. Aside from the Cromwell matter, conclusions about their growing animosity are based largely on private observations they made about each other in their correspondence and journals. It is true that such remarks were often sharp and sometimes almost malicious. Carlyle, in a letter to Lady Ashburton, virtually renounced their friendship, and Emerson in his journal compared Carlyle to a "cunning" St. Peter, who denies friends, books, his own acts, "and immediately the cock crows." The Carlyles' affection for Emerson, Joseph Slater decides, "cooled into something between disenchantment and mocking repudiation," while Emerson's attitude toward Carlyle reached a point beyond which "bitterness could hardly go, and friendship hardly survive."

I believe it is wrong to think of Emerson's second visit with Carlyle primarily in terms of "fundamental disagreements," "quarrels," and "profound alterations of friendship." Interpretations of that sort suggest to me a conception of friendship as all bland harmony, with no discord or confrontation whatever. Emerson had a quite different idea of the meaning of friendship, which he had expressed in an essay years before his trip:

> Friendship requires that rare mean betwixt likeness and unlikeness that piques each with the presence of power and of consent in the other party . . . I hate, where I looked for a manly furtherance or at least a manly resistance, to find a mush of concession. Better be a nettle in the side of your friend than his echo . . . Let it be an alliance of two large, formidable natures, mutually beheld, mutually feared, before yet they recognize the deep identity which, beneath these disparities, unites them. (EW 2:208-209)

From the beginning, from Craigenputtock, the Carlyle-Emerson relationship had never been all affability, and throughout their correspondence there were differences of opinion and occasional sorties, more or less amiably intended, against each other's position on a variety of topics. Since they knew from their letters and their writings so much about each other's ideas and temperaments, when they finally met again they were fully prepared to take each other's measure as mature men.

When they did meet again, Emerson was immediately surprised not by anything Carlyle said but rather by the way he said it. "You will never discover his real vigor & range," he wrote his wife from Chelsea, "or how much more he might do than he has ever done, without seeing him." He did not talk like an intellectual but like "a very practical Scotchman," like the educated peasant he originally was; Emerson was reminded of his own gardener. (He supposed he had missed this quality at Craigenputtock because of the briefness of his visit, but it is also possible that Carlyle's earthiness, not to mention his accent, had become ever more pronounced during his years in London. Emerson was one of the few people who saw him in both places.) He also admired Carlyle's conduct "when he is with fine people," which Emerson compared to the confident manner of Daniel Webster. Carlyle was respected enough that he "can see 'Society' on his own terms."[2] Emerson appreciated outspokenness, and he was clearly impressed by the man's temerity when, several months later, amidst growing anxiety over the situation in France, he heard him deliver a jeremiad against the British aristocracy at a dinner party crowded with British aristocrats. The aristocrats paid no heed other than proposing Carlyle for Parliament as a means of shutting him up. Emerson himself had not lost all faith in the nobility, but he liked to see a man stand up for what he believed was right regardless of whom he might offend. Occasionally he did become annoyed at Carlyle's endless vituperation; he wrote his wife that all Carlyle's "methods involve a good deal of killing, & he does not see his way very clearly or far." But he enjoyed watching Carlyle the peasant shock the smug, myopic English upper classes, and his usual reaction seems to have been one of amusement. "What a fine fellow you are," he once said to him, "to bespatter the world with this oil of vitriol!" Describing his London lectures, he told of his anticipation of having Carlyle in the audience, for "there might be fun: who knew?" But, alas, "no harm was done, no knives were concealed in the words, more is the pity!" — not that he wanted Carlyle to break up the meeting, though he might have preferred it to what happened at another lecture, when the platform committee seated Carlyle directly behind him, staring at the back of his neck.

On balance, I do not feel that Emerson was ever greatly distressed by the antics of his "practical Scotchman." (Incidentally, Carlyle lived up to another aspect of the national stereotype in a note he sent to Emerson in England, instructing the American how to avoid overpaying postage: "How many additional pence," he snorted, in exasperation over his friend's extravagance, "flung away in this manner, may you have given the Queen since you came among us!") He was surprised by some aspects of Carlyle's character, such as his earthiness and the virulence of his conversation. However, he was aware before his visit of Carlyle's inhospitable attitude toward people with ideas different from his own, a crucial trait of his mature personality. And he knew in advance what sort of reception to anticipate in Chelsea.

He knew what to anticipate because he knew what sort of reception the Carlyles had given to others. Much of the Carlyle-Emerson correspondence consists of letters of introduction, most of them from Emerson to Carlyle. Is is conceivable that some part of the Carlyles' ambivalence toward Emerson and toward Americans in general was a consequence of the steady stream of tourists in Chelsea bearing credentials from Concord. After counting "fourteen of them in one fortnight," Jane Carlyle told her uncle in 1843 that "these Yankees form a considerable item in the ennuis of our mortal life."[3] Not that all fourteen "congratulatory Yankees" could be blamed on Emerson, but it was almost inevitable that the association would be made anyway. It was also inevitable that at times Carlyle's fragile patience would shatter in the presence of a visitor. When that happened, Emerson could hear of it not only from the affronted American, but sometimes, in egregious instances, from Carlyle himself. Without question the most egregious instance, one which in the absence of everything else would have alerted Emerson more than adequately to the perils before him, was the visit to number 5 Great Cheyne Row of that flower child of the nineteenth century, A. Bronson Alcott.

Carlyle first heard of Alcott in 1837. "A man named Bronson Alcott," Emerson wrote, pretentiously, at the close of a letter, "is great & one of the jewels we have to show you. Goodbye" (L, p. 163). Still more affected is a description of Alcott in 1839 as "a majestic soul with whom conversation is possible. He is capable of truth, & gives me the same glad astonishment that he should exist which the world does" (p.

218). A year later Alcott was welcomed to Concord to live as "a great man if he cannot write well" (p. 269). By 1842, when the great man was planning a trip to England, Emerson had learned enough about Carlyle's gruff nature to prepare him very carefully for Alcott's visit. First he told Carlyle to forget everything he may have heard or read about Alcott, including his own writings and presumably Emerson's effusive letters. Let him make "a new & primary impression," he requested, without offering an assurance that the impression would be positive. "You may love him, or hate him, or apathetically pass by him, as your genius shall dictate," and with that he left "contentedly my pilgrim to his fate" (p. 320). Emerson was actually using Alcott's trip as an experiment to discover more about both men, as a letter he wrote to John Sterling makes clear (p. 322n). "My friend Alcott must have visited you before this," he reminded Carlyle a few months later, "and you have seen whether any relation could subsist between men so differently excellent" (p. 323). The results of the experiment were soon forthcoming.

Carlyle's first letter about Alcott confirmed what Emerson must have at least suspected, that the two "differ, so far as I can yet compute, from the very centre." For Emerson's sake, Carlyle tried his best to sympathize with the "genial, innocent, simple-hearted man," who had already been there twice "at considerable length; the second time, all night," discoursing on "his one topic," vegetarianism (p. 326). The experiment ended with a third meeting, at which Alcott had to contend with another carnivore (in fact, a lapsed vegetarian), Robert Browning, along with Carlyle. After Browning departed, Alcott answered Carlyle's inquiry, " 'When shall I see you again?' by a solemn 'Never, I guess!' " Carlyle declared that his "whole heart" was "kindly affected" toward Alcott yet and that he wanted to see more of him, although he esteemed "his Potatoe-gospel a mere imbecillity which *cannot* be discussed in this busy world at this time of day" (pp. 329-330). Back in Concord, Emerson had heard enough. "As for Alcott," he wrote Carlyle, "you have discharged your conscience of him manfully & knightly: I absolve you well." He still considered Alcott "a great man" but agreed that he had been carried away by "this eating better than his neighbors" (p. 331).

As might be expected, Alcott's version is significantly different; according to him the source of conflict was not vegetarianism, but Cromwell, the very issue on which Emerson would clash with Carlyle in 1847. Though Alcott wrote little about Carlyle directly to Emerson, he described the argument about Cromwell in a letter to Mrs. Alcott intended for Emerson as well; he advised her that "Emerson will sadden when you tell him what I write." The section that would sadden Emerson is Alcott's description of Carlyle as "sombre, severe, hopeless." He had said to Carlyle that instead of resurrecting Cromwell he was descending into the grave with him (like a potato, perhaps). Whatever remark Emerson made about Cromwell five years later, it could hardly have been more provocative to Carlyle. "The man is sick," Alcott concluded, "he needs rest; he must get that Book off his brain."[4]

The discrepancies between the two versions are of little moment; Emerson would have assessed the accuracy of each man's account from his own perspective. He also would have drawn conclusions about the safest manner of getting along in Chelsea, in hope of preserving the peace and furthering international amity. He must have realized long before he sailed that there would be disagreements; most likely he also understood enough about Carlyle's personality to know that he would readily explode the least difference, and especially a difference about Cromwell, into a schism "as deep as the pit." If he had underestimated Carlyle's argumentative disposition, experience would soon have taught him better. "Carlyle," he wrote from London to an old friend, "always begins with a contradiction."[5] Faithful to the philosophy of his essay on "Friendship," his strategy in dealing with Carlyle was not to avoid contradiction, for he welcomed a true meeting of minds and the contention of ideas. But he felt he could forestall the escalation of controversy into conflagration without having to serve up "a mush of concession." His main tactic was simply to avoid taking offense at Carlyle's remarks. Because of his pacific nature and force of will, and because of his love for his friend, he could maintain his composure before the fulminating Carlyle even at the peak of an eruption. An illustration of the "Friendship" philosophy in action comes from Carlyle himself, who told his Irish friend Gavan Duffy that when he and Emerson "came to talk with each other their opinions were constantly found to clash." After supplying Duffy with vague examples, he went on to say that Emerson "bore, however, with great good humour the utter negation and contradiction of his theories. He had a sharp perking little face, and he kept bobbing it up and down with 'Yissir, yissir' (*mimicking*) in answer to objections or expositions."[6] The comic imitation adds to the ring of truth in Duffy's reminiscence. Carlyle may not have realized what Emerson was doing, but his remarks to Duffy confirm Emerson's success.

Part of the credit, though, should go to the Carlyles themselves, who never lost sight of Emerson's best qualities even when they found him most bothersome. Their ambivalent feelings toward him sometimes bordered on the paradoxical. The letter from Carlyle to Lady Harriet, where he swore that he and Emerson could never be friends, is matched by a letter to the same correspondent from Jane Carlyle. The two letters are similar with respect to Emerson — both comparing him to a reed, for example — and since they were written at about the same time, they may be taken together as the consensus of husband and wife. Jane's sarcasm about "this Yankee seraph" is, if anything, more extreme than her husband's; after listening to him for two days, she told Lady Harriet, she felt like soaking her head in cold water. But further along, the letter offers another glimpse of Emerson keeping the peace and provides as well a revealing insight into the Carlyles' divided perception of him:

Polite and gentle, this Emerson certainly is; he avoids with a laudable tact, all occasions of dispute, and when dragged into it by the hair of his head (morally speaking) he *gives* under the most provoking contradictions, with the softness of a feather-bed.

For the rest, I hardly know what to think of him, or whether I like him or not. The man has *two* faces to begin with which are continually changing into one another like *dissolving views,* the one young, refined, almost beautiful, radiant with what shall I say—"virtue its own reward"! the other decidedly old, hatchet-like, crotchety, inconclusive, like an incarnation of one of his own poems.[7]

It is unlikely that by saying Emerson "gives" under pressure Jane meant that he breaks and runs, for she was describing (though her letter does not mention) the period of the Cromwell skirmish. Nor do I believe that by saying he had two faces she meant that he was two-faced; actually her odd description is expressive, in my opinion, of her apprehension of the complexity of Emerson's character.

"Of one impression we fail not here," Carlyle wrote Emerson after the latter's return to Concord, "admiration of your pacific virtues, of gentle and noble tolerance, often *sorely* tried in this place!" (L, p. 443). I do not deny that Carlyle and Emerson argued, disagreed, and perhaps quarreled during Emerson's visit. They were both strong-minded men who took their convictions seriously. Their ideas most often differed, sometimes widely and profoundly, with regard to politics, which is always a volatile subject. There were also important national differences; they were citizens of countries which, after all, had twice been at war in the preceding century and had almost gone to war again in a boundary dispute just a year of two before Emerson's trip. ("Is it likely," Carlyle wrote in 1846, "we shall meet in 'Oregon,' think you? That would be a beautiful affair, on the part of the most enlightened Nation!") But in spite of all their differences it is possible to say both of these two writers and of their countries that their beliefs share many common premises, that their outlooks have similar perspectives, and that even at their most distant they are always in many ways united. Perhaps that is too clever to be true, but it is undeniable that the respect, sympathy, and friendship of Carlyle and Emerson for each other survived and strengthened while Emerson was in England. In the years that followed they embraced opposing causes but never doubted that in sincerity and in goodness of heart they were yet as one. "Forgive me my ferocities," Carlyle's letter continues, "you do not quite know what I suffer in these latitudes, or perhaps it would be even easier for you." Emerson did not respond to Carlyle's apology and explanation. Apparently he felt it unnecessary; everything was understood.

Carlyle was not a great political thinker; yet his influence was extraordinary because of the remarkable variety of political theorists who were attracted to him (and still are). In fact, his presence was strongest in political philosophies most antagonistic to each other, as the following pair of excerpts illustrate. In the first one, the *Communist Manifesto* of 1848, the authors declared that the bourgeoisie

has pitilessly torn asunder the motley ties that bound man to his "natural superiors," and has left remaining no other nexus between man and man than naked self-interest, than callous "cash payment." It has drowned the most heavenly ecstasies of religious fervor . . . in the icy water of egotistical calculation. It has resolved personal worth into exchange value and, in place of the numberless indefeasible chartered freedoms, has set up that single, unconscionable freedom — free trade.[8]

Although Carlyle would not have enclosed "natural superiors" and "religious fervor" in sardonic quotation marks (visible or putative), he would have agreed with the sentiments because he had been expressing them for years. The *Manifesto* obliquely acknowledges the debt by the quotation marks around "cash payment." The expropriation of his language by Marx and Engels was not coincidental, of course, for Marx's young disciple was a warm admirer of Carlyle and had cited him frequently and to good effect in an earlier work, *The Condition of the Working Class in England in 1844.*[9]

Unlike the *Communist Manifesto,* the other document was forgotten within a few decades of its publication in 1857, but as the major work of a leading apologist for American slavery, it was widely read at the time. The name of the book is *Cannibals All! or Slaves Without Masters,* and the author, George Fitzhugh, loudly proclaimed Carlyle's writings as the inspiration for his title and subtitle as well as for much of his thinking. Here is his comparison of the lot of the free laborer with that of the slave:

> Capital exercises a more perfect compulsion over free labor-
> ers than human masters over slaves; for free laborers must at all
> times work or starve, and slaves are supported whether they
> work or not. Free laborers have less liberty than slaves, are
> worse paid and provided for, and have no valuable rights . . .
> Though each free laborer has no particular master, his wants
> and other men's capital make him a slave without a master, or
> with too many masters, which is as bad as none. It were often
> better that he had an ascertained master, instead of an irre-
> sponsible and unascertained one.[10]

Fitzhugh's defense of slavery and Marx and Engels's critique of the bourgeoisie both share with Carlyle a radical reinter-pretation of the meaning of "freedom." Ideally defined as "the ability to control one's destiny," in a society based on money the real meaning of freedom is economic: "the ability to buy and sell property freely, including one's labor and that of others." In theory everyone has free choice about his own life; in practice those without money are without choice because they are dependent on those with money for the means of existence. Thus when Marx and Engels call free trade the "unconscionable freedom" and Fitzhugh speaks of slavery "without a master," they are talking about the same contradiction, epitomized by Carlyle in the phrase, "liberty to die by starvation." The Confederate, the Communists, and Carlyle agree more or less in their analysis of bourgeois freedom; they differ, philosophically at least, on what they want to replace it.

But to which camp did Carlyle belong? Was he a progressive or a reactionary, a leftist or a rightist, a crypto-communist or a proto-fascist? The question of his political allegiance is as debatable in the twentieth century as it was in the nineteenth. The controversy has helped keep his name alive, though often for reasons largely extraneous to the man and his work. During the thirties and forties, for example, a few German professors sought to enshrine him as a precursor of National Socialism, and a few anti-Nazis, notably Eric Bentley, seemed willing and almost grateful for the opportunity to dispose of the puzzling ambiguities in Carlyle's career by conceding him to the Reich. The tendency of more recent criticism has been to drag him back toward the left. In 1962 Georg Lukács wrote a new preface to *The Theory of the Novel,* which refers in passing to *Past and Present* as "a preliminary form of a socialist critique."[11] By playing off Carlyle against Marx and Nietzsche in the latter part of *Carlyle and the Idea of the Modern,* Albert J. La-Valley achieved a complicated portrait of Carlyle as a social prophet; because of his "multiplicity" he could sound like Marx and Nietzsche almost simultaneously. LaValley's book is thorough and persuasive but leaves an impression of Carlyle as a somewhat fractured personality, a consequence, perhaps, of LaValley's determination to make him seem "modern." The latest study of his political thought, Philip Rosenberg's *The Seventh Hero,* places him further on the left than anyone had since the young Engels, and his subtitle proclaims at the outset his belief that a "theory of radical activism" is inherent in Carlyle's work.

The traditional explanation for Carlyle's erratic politics might be called "biological hindsight"; it claims that he started out as a youthful progressive and grew more and more conservative with age. Engels introduced a variation of the theory by finding a watershed event in Carlyle's development. He altered a note to the first edition of *Condition of the Working Class,* which praised the "Germanophile Englishman" for his social criticism, in order to inform readers of later editions that the French Revolution of 1848 "turned Carlyle into a complete reactionary. His righteous anger against the philistines turned into a sour-grapes, philistine-like peevishness at the wave of history which had left him stranded."[12] Many critics follow Engels in locating the metamorphosis somewhere in that period, though usually without so precise a turning point. In his bibliography of Carlyle, G. B. Tennyson is justly suspicious of such approaches because they license the critic's own prejudices by enabling him "to select what he likes of Carlyle and reject what he does not by positing the good as early and the bad as late; between the two occurs a souring and hardening on Carlyle's part that renders him distasteful in old age." Tennyson feels that the "bifurcated" method is endemic to Carlyle studies, biographical and critical, old and new.[13]

No one would dispute that he was rather conservative in his old age and radical in his youth. What is questionable is the popular assumption, whether stated or implied, that around 1850 he suddenly flip-flopped, turned topsy-turvy politically, and grew ancient overnight. He himself did not see his life that way; to be specific, he never renounced the radicalism of his youth. Proponents of Carlyle the young revolutionary are fond of an anecdote in his *Reminiscences* about social unrest in 1819, when he was just twenty-four. An acquaintance who had volunteered to help put down radical workers in Glasgow advised him to get a musket, and Carlyle remembered telling the man that he had not "yet quite settled on which side" he cared to fight, which, he added, "really expressed my feeling."[14] As it happens, a letter he wrote to his brother at the time describing the same events makes no mention of this particular incident,[15] but in his old age he recalled his radical sentiments of almost fifty years earlier rather fondly, albeit a little disapprovingly, but without denunciation or apology. He and his friends, "all of us juniors," shared "a sense that revolt against such a load of unveracities, impostures, and quietly inane formalities would one day become indispensable." And although he had since come to realize that their excitement was "rash, false, and quasi-insolent . . . , revolt being a light matter to the young," he could still recognize the "emphasis of sincerity" in the "little crowd" he had heard on that December day in 1819 inviting the militia to go to the devil. He never pictured himself as a foolish young firebrand who later saw through the irrationality of his passions before it was too late. To be sure, he had learned that revolt was not a light matter, but neither were oppression and injustice.

The dichotomy between the young progressive and the old reactionary cannot account for the simple fact that he expressed ideas which come under both labels throughout his life. In 1834, years before he wrote the "radical" books like *Chartism* and *Past and Present,* he argued with John Sterling, the very first time they met, about slavery. Sterling suggested, "with a kindly jeer," that Carlyle consult black people themselves before consigning them to an "engagement for life" (CW 11:106). ("Sterling's notions," Carlyle blandly commented in his *Life of Sterling,* "had not advanced into the stage of mine.") On the other hand, in 1871, long after the "conservative" *Latter-Day Pamphlets* and *Frederick the Great,* he described for his brother in Canada the animosity against the rich on the part of British workers, especially the "higher kinds of them," and predicted that "before many years the huge abominable Boil will *burst,* and the British Empire fall into convulsions."[16] Sometimes he could sound like a revolutionary or a reactionary at different places in the same book; a good example is his thinking on the philosophical nature of insurrection in *Chartism.* At one point he exclaimed that "a permanent Injustice even from an Infinite Power would prove unendurable by men," whose "only resource" against such a "blind No-God, of Necessity and Mechanism . . . would be, with or without hope, — *revolt*" (CW 29:146). But elsewhere obedience is declared "the primary duty of man." "Rebel, without due and most due cause, is the ugliest of words"; and he added, as if fearful that his earlier statement might be misconstrued, that "the first rebel was Satan" (p. 189). Revolt is justified, even glorified, but only under metaphysical provocation.

Carlyle would not have acknowledged a contradiction between his early and late ideas or an ambivalence in his thought at any period, and, on his own terms, he would be right. There is no willful illogicality in his thinking; the logic is often doubtful, but it is always comprehensible. Championship of the oppressed poor, he might say, does not necessarily conflict with slavery because the poor require strong government to overcome their poverty. Should Britain collapse into class warfare, the upper classes would deserve their fate not because they asserted their privileges but because they failed to provide powerful leadership. Revolution is divine when justified, diabolic when not. Such concepts may not be valid but they are not inconsistent; nor was he the first or the last to think them.

Although he was not inconsistent, he was profoundly ambivalent, but his ambivalence had its genesis in his emotions rather than in his ideology and found its greatest expression artistically rather than philosophically. His dreams and passions forced themselves upon his writings, transforming the artistic effect and sometimes reversing the ostensible meaning. Examine the theory of history in *Sartor Resartus*. Teufelsdröckh borrows from Goethe the doctrine of an alternation of ages, from belief to unbelief and back again (*SR*, p. 112). Cyclic theories of history involving growth and decay were common in the nineteenth century; the particular tradition to which Carlyle adhered differs from others mainly because, in René Wellek's words, it posits "an unpredictable development" and its "goal is vague and uncertain."[17] The difference Wellek identifies becomes highly significant when Teufelsdröckh changes the historical theory into the artistic symbol of the phoenix. Like the phoenix, society continually dies and is reborn as the human race proceeds through history, but since Carlyle envisioned no particular destination or ultimate purpose, he was as happy to witness the symbolic destruction of the old as he was to contemplate the creation of the new. The Editor explains that Teufelsdröckh is "content that old sick Society should be deliberately burnt" because he has "faith that she is a Phoenix; and that a new heavenborn young one will rise out of her ashes," but the Professor's own exhilarated language betrays a far greater eagerness for the burning than for the rising. "When the Phoenix is fanning her funeral pyre," he chortles, "will there not be sparks flying! Alas," he goes on, the ancient word of lament not quite in keeping with the tone, "some millions of men . . . have already been licked into that high-eddying Flame, and like moths consumed there. Still also have we to fear that incautious beards will get singed" (*SR*, pp. 236-237). The sarcastic last sentence reflects the ecstatic celebration of fire inherent in the phoenix symbol.

At the conclusion of *The French Revolution* Carlyle's pyrophilia becomes apocalyptic; here his mouthpiece is "the Arch-quack Cagliostro," who prophesies the Revolution:

> IMPOSTURE is in flames, Imposture is burnt up: one red sea of Fire, wild-billowing, enwraps the World: with its fire-tongue licks at the very Stars. Thrones are hurled into it, and Dubois Mitres, and Prebendal Stalls that drop fatness, and—ha! what see I?—all the *Gigs* of Creation: all, all!. . . RESPECTABILITY, with all her collected Gigs inflamed for funeral pyre, wailing, leaves the Earth . . . The Images all run into amorphous Corinthian brass: all Dwellings of men destroyed; the very mountains peeled and riven, the valleys black and dead: it is an empty World! Woe to them that shall be born then! . . . For it is the End of the dominion of IMPOSTURE (which is darkness and opaque Fire-damp); and the burning up, with unquenchable fire, of all the Gigs that are in the Earth. (CW 4: 322-323)

By the burning of gigs Carlyle meant the destruction of the idle upper classes; he coined the words "gigmen" and "gig-manity" as a sneering synecdoche for "gentlemen" and so overused the term that even Emerson complained (L, p. 161). Carlyle would defend the torching of rotten structures as a precondition for the laying of new foundations. The phoenix must be consumed before it can be reborn. But the truth is that Carlyle loved to watch it burn.

In his comments on the *French Revolution* volumes in his *Westminster* article on Carlyle, John Sterling spoke of "a hatred for things as they are, showing itself in cool mockery at their destruction, and in joy at manifestations, however monstrous, of the will to destroy them."[18] Speaking on behalf of Carlyle the revolutionary, Philip Rosenberg answers Sterling's accusation by countercharging that Sterling's attitude betrays his "class bias." War is deplorable, Rosenberg argues, class war not excepted, but it is unfair to call Carlyle perverse because he refused to condemn the atrocities of the Sansculottes more vehemently than the oppression by the ruling class which provoked them.[19] Though it is true that in his essay Sterling sympathized with the Ancien Régime and regretted Carlyle's admiration for Danton,[20] his opinions should not be dismissed as the peeve of a fastidious Tory. (Whatever his "class bias," we have seen how Sterling's feelings on slavery compared with Carlyle's "advanced" views!) Carlyle did love destruction for its own sake. The attraction was mainly esthetic, and with his feel for the beauty of chaos and conflagration he created art of overpowering intensity, as in the conclusion of *The French Revolution*. The images run together and flow in molten streams: the wind whips the blazing sea and the burning waves become red tongues that caress the flickering stars; the mountains peel from the heat and blacken the valleys; and all the while fueling the inferno are the ludicrous symbols of human dignity and righteousness: the king's throne, the bishop's headdress, church furniture dripping fat from the seats, and finally the gentleman's gig—now, perhaps, become a phaeton.

His obsession with order followed from his passion for chaos and destruction. He believed that humanity itself was a destructive power that could be restrained only by a collective act of will; when the will is lacking, chaos follows inevitably. In *The French Revolution* he went further than Hobbes in declaring the state of nature to be not just a state of war but a state of "Cannibalism: That *I* can devour *Thee*"; such was his answer to Rousseau's *Contrat Social* (CW 2:55). He may have differed from Hobbes in his assumption that man is fundamentally a social animal, but he believed that the primary, instinctual social grouping is the mob, "a genuine outburst of Nature." "The thing they will do is known to no man," he wrote in connection with the women's mobs in Paris, "least of all to themselves. It is the inflammablest immeasurable Firework, generating, consuming itself" (p. 251). Along with their nerve, and eventually their heads, the rulers of France lost the will to order. Deprived of leadership, the mass of the population took refuge in the only form of social organization open to them: they formed a national mob.

Carlyle's conception of society, like his conception of the individual, is based on freedom of will. His theory of history is in a sense deterministic, for the alternation of epochs, the endlessly recurring death and rebirth of the phoenix, proceeds as inexorably as the passage of time itself. But since there is no ultimate destination or even a guarantee that the new era will constitute an improvement over its predecessors, society is always faced with the choice of working for a better world in the future or, almost literally, letting it all go to hell. I do not agree with Philip Rosenberg when, following Carlyle's contemporary, the Italian revolutionist Mazzini, he detects a "nihilistic strain" in Carlyle founded on the suspicion that regardless of human endeavor the "forces of annihilation" will triumph anyway.[21] The outcome is doubtful precisely because humanity is free to choose. Carlyle often spoke of history as a "revelation" or a "Bible," which vaguely implies a preordained divine plan; the same might be said of the "Tree Igdrasil" in the *Heroes* book. But in "On History

Again" (1833), a brief "Inaugural Discourse" delivered by
"D. T." to the "Society for the Diffusion of Common Hon-
esty," he suggested a theory of history in which humanity
writes its own program. Instead of a parchment from
heaven, history is "the Letter of Instructions, which the old
generations write and posthumously transmit to the new;
nay, it may be called, more generally still, the Message, verbal or written, which all Mankind delivers to every man"
(CW 28:167). History is what the human race has made of
its existence in the past, and the purpose of historiography is
to clarify the lessons of the past for those engaged in creating the present and the future.

Society is free to choose between order and anarchy, but
as he aged Carlyle became more and more convinced that
society's wish for order could be achieved and maintained
only through the beneficent rule of a dictator (or, if you prefer Rosenberg's euphemism, a "charismatic leader"). Democracy would not do because a society committed to democracy is not firmly committed to anything in Carlyle's
sense. Democracy is not so much an evil as a blind alley. In
the "Organic Filaments" chapter of *Sartor Resartus,* Teufelsdröckh deliberately contradicts himself on the virtues
and failings of democracy; the confused Editor is happy to
leave the "labyrinths" and turn to hero worship (*SR,* p.
250). Carlyle, it seems, acted the same way. One reason for
dictatorship is that by rallying to a leader, society attains
both a symbol and an embodiment of the collective will to
order. Rosenberg intends something along these lines with
his "theory of radical activism," and I think Carlyle would
have approved of much of what Rosenberg says.[22] But there
was also an important psychological advantage for Carlyle
in his glorification of dictators in general, and of certain
dictators in particular. His favorite dictators were both violent rebels and violent rulers, and they enabled him to grat-
ify his craving for order and direction and at the same time
satisfy his illicit passion for rebellion and destruction.

The obvious example is Cromwell, who overthrew the

established order and executed the legitimate ruler. But Carlyle was not content for Cromwell merely to found a new order and become the new legitimate ruler; his Cromwell must also remain a fighter. Originally he had rebelled against corruption in the name of order, and once in control he continued to battle corruption, only now from the top rather than from the bottom. His dismissal of the Rump Parliament in a way constituted a sort of rebellion from the top. Carlyle, following his usual biographical procedure, "reported" Cromwell's words to the Rump Parliament "in clear blaze of conflagration": " 'Corrupt unjust persons; scandalous to the profession of the Gospel': how can you be a Parliament for God's People? Depart, I say; and let us have done with you. In the name of God, —go!" (CW 8:35). Similarly Dr. Francia, the Paraguayan dictator celebrated by Carlyle in an essay of 1843, maintained his authority through a reign of terror (though Carlyle insisted that, as reigns of terror go, Francia's was not all that terrible). The hero of *Past and Present,* Abbot Samson, had to lead the forces of order against "relaxed lazy monks, not disinclined to mutiny in mass," and he, too, instituted a kind of terror:

> Wheresoever Disorder may stand or lie, let it have a care; here is the man that has declared war with it, that never will make peace with it. Man is the Missionary of Order; he is the servant not of the Devil and Chaos, but of God and the Universe! Let all sluggards, and cowards, remiss, false-spoken, unjust, and otherwise diabolic persons have a care: this is a dangerous man for them. (CW 10:91-92)

The "Missionary of Order" is hardly a man of peace, and Carlyle's criteria for order clearly do not include the absence of violence or the threat of violence. His adoption of the slogan "might makes right" shoud be considered in this context, though it should be emphasized that he certainly was not endorsing sheer force. As C. F. Harrold points out, he "made the reservation that Might must first be Right in

order to '*make*' Right."²³ Still, his delight in violence is unmistakable, and his ability to depict violence was virtually
the one literary skill he possessed which did not decline
toward the end of his career. Only the varieties of violent
action change, as scenes of street fighting in Paris are replaced by panoramas of formal battles in Central Europe,
about all that is still worth reading in the dreary *History of
Frederick the Great*.

The army succeeds the mob in yet another sense. Carlyle's
dichotomy between order and anarchy admitted no middle
ground, and as his opinions hardened he tended to place the
two extremes further apart, until his ultimate vision of the
social order was a society under militaristic regimentation.
It is tempting to account for his authoritarian programs as
reflections of his medievalism or his nostalgia for Cromwell's
New Model Army, but actually his prescription for a hier-
archically ordered society came from the present and not
the past. He recognized that a large part of the population
had already undergone regimentation through the growth
of modern industry; he also recognized the promise of technology to transform the world. At one point in *Chartism*
(1839), the reader is asked whether he regards Manchester,
the capital of the Industrial Revolution, "with its cotton-
fuzz, its smoke and dust, its tumult and contentious squalor," as hideous. He should not, for hidden beneath the
ugliness is something "beautiful as magic dreams and yet no
dream but a reality." What is potentially so beautiful is the
thought of a vast industrial army building the future:

> Hast thou heard, with sound ears, the awakening of a Man-
> chester, on Monday morning, at half-past five by the clock; the
> rushing off of its thousand mills, like the boom of an Atlantic
> tide, ten thousand times ten thousand spools and spindles all
> set humming there . . .? Cotton-spinning is the clothing of the
> naked in its result; the triumph of man over matter in its
> means. Soot and despair are not the essence of it; they are divis-
> ible from it, — at this hour, are they not crying fiercely to be
> divided? (CW 29:181-182)²⁴

Here is the germ of his proposal for "Industrial Regiments," commanded by "Captains of Industry," remaking Britain, and through emigration conquering and enriching the world. The latter, imperial variation on the regimental theme is first sounded in *Sartor* and expanded in *Chartism,* which ends with a call for "an Emigrant host larger than Xerxes," equipped "with the steamengine and plough-share," to settle the ninety percent of the globe which, according to Carlyle's estimate, is crying out for inhabitants.

He had great difficulty in deciding who should actually organize the industrial armies, at home and abroad. Generally he looked to the capitalists, especially in *Past and Present,* but sometimes he called forth the aristocracy, provided they would give up game-preserving; occasionally he invoked the power of the state and even held out hope for Parliament. Finally, in the *Latter-Day Pamphlets* (1850), he settled on a formula whereby some industries would be controlled by the state and others by private capital, like a fanciful cross between Lenin's New Economic Policy and Roosevelt's New Deal, for each sector would encourage the growth of the other. The plan is fuzzy, to say the least, but one aspect is salient. The structuring and regimenting of society must increase until it becomes universal: "Thus will all Masters of Workmen, private Captains of Industry, be forced to incessantly cooperate with the State and its public Captains; they regimenting in their way, the State in its way, with ever-widening field." The ultimate goal is a nation in which "there be no unregimented worker, or such only as are fit to remain unregimented, any more" (CW 20:166).

It is hard to imagine his obsession with order going still further, but in "Shooting Niagara: And After?" (1867), his last major political statement (touched off by the second Reform Bill), he proposed some sort of "military Drill," with an actual "Drill-Sergeant," for "the entire Population," so that everyone could experience "the silent charm of rhythmic human companionship" (CW 30:40-43).[25] Such a fantasy goes beyond the categories of left- and right-wing politics; Mao's China and Hitler's Germany both fail as anal-

ogies for this nightmare of a nation of rhythmic automa-
tons. Not surprisingly in view of the state of mind the article
suggests, that part of it ends with the prophecy of a "duel to
the death" between "Anarchy and Anti-ditto," as if the two
abstractions were actually opposing armies (as in Twain's
Connecticut Yankee). His compulsion about order and
chaos finally caused him completely to lose sight of
humanity.

The bitter irony of his lifelong drift toward an ever more
absolute authoritarianism, and his consequent insensitivity
to the simplest human traits, is that he sincerely believed all
his ideas proceeded from his love and pity for the human
race, and not for some grand abstract entity (the thought
would have repelled him), but for real human beings. A
concern for people, he felt, not only inspired his own work
but accounted for its artistic success as well; as he explained
in the essay "Biography," a writer must begin with "an open
loving heart." "Other secret for being 'graphic' is there
none, worth having: but this is an all-sufficient one" (CW
28:57). And in truth there is nothing that more decisively
rescues him from condemnation either as a would-be Hitler
or as a would-be Robespierre than the undeniable compassion which pervades his early and middle work and never
entirely disappears. In the same article that denounced his
infatuation with violence, John Sterling also elevated Carlyle
over all other writers with regard to his "passionate sorrow"
for the common people throughout history; their sufferings,
Sterling wrote, "press upon his soul like personal calami-
ties."[26]

Carlyle saw himself as a partisan of the lower classes; he
claimed to write on their behalf. He would not join the Anti-
Corn Law League, he wrote his brother Alexander in 1842,
because "I am already engaged for a far bigger *League,*" the
league "of the oppressed Poor against the idle Rich."[27] The
phrase encapsules the antithetical tendencies of his politics.
He was a revolutionary, prepared to fight against oppression, but he was also a conservative, opposed to the rich not
because of their wealth but because of their idleness. Here is

the young man who could not decide whether to use his musket against the rebellious workers or against the militia raised to suppress them. The poor always have the right (as well as the might) to oppose an unjust society and to demand that their leaders work for a better society. And to Carlyle, a just society meant an ordered society.

He believed that all society was, or should be, a family. The idea was not just a metaphor to him. In large families (such as his parents' family) each member has an obligation to help the others with support, advice, guidance, and, if necessary, through stern correction. The strong should aid the weak, the wise instruct the foolish. The foulest sin a family could commit would be to disown a family member; such a crime would reveal the family's disintegration and presage its destruction. That holds true for society as a whole, and he found an incident to illustrate the point in a report on poverty in Scotland published in 1840. (Engels used the same report in *The Condition of the Working Class,* but he was more concerned with the economics and the statistics than with the anecdotes.)[28] In the chapter of *Past and Present* entitled "Gospel of Mammonism," he tells of a "poor Irish Widow" of Edinburgh, a literary descendant of Wordsworth's Martha Ray and an ancestor of Arnold's Wragg, whose husband dies leaving her and her children destitute. The "Charitable Establishments" refuse to help, so she dies of typhus, in the process spreading the infection and causing seventeen more deaths. " 'I am your sister,' " she cries, " 'bone of your bone; one God made us: ye must help me!' " But society denies the relationship, saying: " 'thou art no sister of ours.' But she proves her sisterhood," Carlyle comments; "her typhus-fever kills *them:* they actually were her brothers, though denying it!" (CW 10:149). What kills her and her persecutors is not mere selfishness and worship of money; Carlyle cites the opinion of the author of the report that it would have been more economical to have saved the woman. The real cause of the deaths is that society was allowing itself to fall apart.

His fear that society was going to pieces, and his conviction that without an ordered society injustice and suffering would increase, inspired the most influential and lasting aspect of his political writing: his critique of laissez-faire, the primary business of his briefest book, *Chartism*. To Carlyle laissez-faire meant anarchy, not anarchy in the sense of irresponsibly allowing everyone freedom, but anarchy caused by the refusal to take responsibility for one's fellow creatures when they are in need. The demands of the poor for strong leadership ("Guide me, govern me!" they cry in *Chartism*) are no different from the appeal of the widow with typhus, and the "abdication" of the governors is no different from the callousness of the Charitable Establishments. The weak and the poor have an unquestionable claim on society to be cared for and to be helped. In the guise of generously granting liberty, laissez-faire actually dissolves the bonds of kinship and hypocritically consigns the poor to misery in the name of freedom. Real freedom, he insisted in the chapter of *Chartism* called "Laissez-faire," is inseparable from the "right of the ignorant man to be guided by the wiser . . . , a sacred right and duty, on both sides; and the summary of all social duties between the two." He would have denied that he insulted the lower classes when he likened them in that chapter to "a dumb creature in rage and pain." He would stress his respect for honest labor and his pity for the worker's plight when he is unemployed, and he would say that all his harshness and wrath are reserved for the upper classes. "The brawny craftsman finds it no child's play to mould his unpliant rugged masses; neither is guidance of men a dilettantism: what it becomes when treated as a dilettantism, we may see!" (CW 29:157-158). Carlyle's readers knew what it becomes: burning wheat stacks and burning gigs. His attitude toward the oppressed poor was, to understate the matter, patronizing, but he hated the idle rich passionately (at least in his writings — he had some wealthy friends). At one point in *Past and Present* he advanced the Maoist proposal that the "Duke of Logwood, now rolling sumptuously" to Parliament in a gig, should be set to ploughing "on seven-and-sixpence a week, with no outdoor relief" — meaning the workhouse should the Duke be laid off (CW 10:89). It should be apparent why his attacks on laissez-faire, here and in later works, had political repercussions on both the left and the right.

His objections to democracy in his later work follow his social analysis. Democracy is the political analogue of laissez-faire economics and the cash nexus and is symptomatic of the breakup of the social family; "translated into practical language," he explained in "The Present Time," the first of the *Latter-Day Pamphlets,* "enfranchisement" and "emancipation" really mean "the cutting asunder of human relations." "Let us all be 'free' of one another," the pamphlet continues sarcastically, "we shall then be happy. Free, without bond or connection except that of cash payment." Soon he reached the heart of the matter: forget about marriage and the family, he proposed, "and now let a new Sacrament, that of *Divorce,* which we call emancipation, and spout-of on our platforms, be universally the order of the day!" (CW 20:24-25). As we have seen, Teufelsdröckh had been undecided about democracy, but Carlyle's opposition became clear at least as early as *Chartism* (cf. pp. 53-55). It came down to this: society is a family, and governors can no more be elected than can parents. (The better known metaphor he actually used in "The Present Time," that of a ship and its captain rounding Cape Horn, does not, in my opinion, very effectively express his own idea; for one thing, it is a blatantly false analogy.) Like a family, society needs caring but commanding leadership, rulers who are both loved and feared by the ruled. In a family parentage is determined biologically, but in the societal family leaders cannot be selected so automatically. But if they cannot be elected democratically, how then can society discover its true leaders? Carlyle's entire political system — to the extent that he had a "system" — failed on that very question, though he had searched for an answer in his finest political book, *Past and Present* (1843).

With *Heroes and Hero-Worship* he hoped that by reviving the memory of leaders from the past and, through artistic means, recreating the immediacy of their appeal, he could teach hero worshippers of the present how to look for the right contemporary leaders. A similar ambition motivated his years of work on Cromwell. But despite his efforts the historical figures remained obstinately in the past. It was a problem recognized by Emerson. "I shall be glad if you will draw Cromwell," he wrote in 1840 after first hearing of the projected biography, "though, if I should choose, it would be Carlyle. You will not feel that you have done your work until those devouring eyes & that portraying hand have achieved England in the Nineteenth Century" (L, p. 283). Emerson may have repeated his advice in 1842 in a letter which is now missing, for it was then that Carlyle responded:

> One of my grand difficulties I suspect to be that I cannot write *two Books at once;* cannot be in the seventeenth century and in the nineteenth at one and the same moment . . . For my heart is sick and sore in behalf of my own poor generation; nay I feel withal as if the one hope of help for it consisted in the possibility of new Cromwells and new Puritans: thus do the two centuries stand related to me, the seventeenth *worthless* except precisely in so far as it can be made the nineteenth; and yet let anybody *try* that enterprise! (L, p. 328)

But Cromwell refused to budge from his century; so at the start of the next year Carlyle set him aside for seven weeks and, working at a white heat, tried the enterprise of uniting the present with the past. He wrote two books at once.

One book is the biography of a leader, the abbot of a medieval monastery; the other book is an analysis of modern British society. Carlyle by now was an experienced practitioner of both genres: he had lectured on heroism and labored over Cromwell; he had confronted the "condition-of-England question" in *Chartism* and in earlier essays. His biographical methods had become more sophisticated and complex than in the *Heroes* book. He still identified with his subject, but he also maintained an esthetic distance which enabled him to step back from time to time and reflect. Various authorial levels intercede between Abbot Samson and the reader: Samson's contemporary and Carlyle's source, Jocelin; the "Editor"; and Carlyle in his own voice with occasional appearances from such favorite mouthpieces as Sauerteig and Teufelsdröckh. In addition to detachment, he achieved some beautiful, almost surreal effects with the distancing device, as when the Editor looks into Jocelin's eyes, "deep as our own, *imaging* our own, but all unconscious of us; to whom we, for the time, are become as spirits and invisible!" (CW 10:50). (A few years later he used a sinister variation of the same technique in his letter about Emerson's daguerreotype.) The advances over *Chartism* are mainly in greater precision and expressiveness of language. He extends the concept of the cash nexus into the epitome of laissez-faire economics in the chapter "Gospel of Mammonism" and elsewhere. And the present hypocritical "misgovernment," for the most part nameless in *Chartism,* comes to life in *Past and Present* through characters such as "my right honourable friend Sir Jabesh Windbag, Mr. Facing-both-ways, Viscount Mealymouth, Earl of Windlestraw" (p. 223).

Writing about two very different ages simultaneously is indeed a daring enterprise, and it is hard to say whether *Past and Present* ultimately succeeds or fails. The element holding together the book about the past and the book about the present is Carlyle's preoccupation with the question of how to find leaders. The opening section, after outlining the problem and rejecting democracy as a solution, ends by suggesting that the puzzle may not be soluble at all. It would be wonderful if "the present Editor" could "instruct men how to know Wisdom, Heroism, when they see it," but the task would require a god-Editor. "Let no Editor hope such things: no; — and yet," he adds, hopefully, "let all Editors aim towards such things, and even towards such alone!" (p. 38). But whatever his hopes, Carlyle could discover no sure way to recognize and install true leaders.

When he comes to the elevation of Samson to abbot after a sort of secret ballot election, he is almost forced to admit that even democracy cannot be ruled out. And he comes close to saying that a society gets the government it deserves regardless of its wishes or its means of expressing them, a position which would render superfluous hero worship itself. What seems to have been his final answer merely rephrases the question: "A heroic people chooses heroes, and is happy; a valet or flunky people chooses sham-heroes, what are called quacks, thinking them heroes, and is not happy" (pp. 75-76). That was the best he could do.

"What is the end of Government?" he asked in the chapter called "Two Centuries." It might have been called "Four Centuries," since along with the past and present of the book it also refers to Cromwell's century and to the future. He answered the question rhetorically at first:

> To guide men in the way wherein they should go; towards their true good in this life, the portal of infinite good in a life to come? To guide men in such a way, and ourselves in such a way, as the Maker of men, whose eye is upon us, will sanction at the Great Day? — Or alas, perhaps at bottom *is* there no Great Day, no sure outlook of any life to come; but only this poor life, and what of taxes, felicities, Nell-Gwynns and entertainments we can muster here? In that case, the end of Government will be, To suppress all noise and disturbance, whether of Puritan preaching, Cameronian psalm-singing, thieves'-riot, murder, arson, or what noise soever, and — be careful that supplies do not fail! (pp. 166-167)

As so often happens with Carlyle, the thought of death caused him to examine his own ideas more critically. Here, I think, for an instant, he pierced the heart of his own politics. If society indeed is a family, then the leaders should rule autocratically because they will exercise their power to guide their followers upward, and they will act only for the sake of love. But if society is not a family — if there is no "Great Day" toward which God the Father guides us — then the kind of strong government Carlyle was advocating would mean nothing but universal repression, for society would comprise a mass of slaves with no purpose other than to stay alive. He wrote *Past and Present* too quickly. If he recognized the nature of his own prophecy when he grimly uttered it, he must have soon forgotten, for his totalitarian vision evolved in later years into the nightmares of the *Latter-Day Pamphlets* and "Shooting Niagara," where "all noise and disturbance" are suppressed with a vengeance.

Yet he could not construct a political system because, regardless how he thought of himself, he was too impractical. It is surprising to realize that a man who prided himself on his work in the real world, and who accused Emerson of being a misty dreamer, produced only one substantial idea for a practical political reform: in the latter-day pamphlet called "Downing Street" he proposed that certain executive positions in government should be appointed and not require a seat in Parliament (CW 20:144ff.).[29] Aside from this modest suggestion (for which the British practice of reserving safe seats for irreplaceable M.P.'s serves much the same purpose), he produced only visions and pipe dreams, at first harmless schemes for industrial regiments and global emigration, then dark fantasies of drillmasters and human machines. Carlyle was always his own Teufelsdröckh.

He also accused Emerson of being isolated, and, as with the charge of impracticality, Emerson cheerfully confessed. But Carlyle was isolated, too, even in London. And though he hated isolation — "the sum-total of wretchedness" he called it in *Past and Present* (p. 274) — he became more out of touch with human reality as his concern for the human condition increased. It was, as I said, a bitter irony. People were all around him, but he was profoundly alone, more alone than he had been at Craigenputtock. His isolation, I think, helped him drift further from reality, hastened his progress toward totalitarianism, and exacerbated his predilection for violence. Emerson saw everything immediately on his second visit to England. "He talks like a very unhappy man," he wrote in his first letter home from Chelsea, "profoundly solitary, displeased & hindered by all men & things about him, & plainly biding his time, & meditating how to undermine & explode the whole world of nonsense which torments him."[30]

Before they began to exchange daguerreotypes, Carlyle and Emerson had already decided to stop acting as each other's transatlantic editor. Despite heroic efforts on both sides of the ocean—with a chronically ill woman in London painfully copying Carlyle's manuscript while lying on her back, then Emerson in Concord deciphering the woman's handwriting before rushing the manuscript and some loose printed sheets to the printer—the authorized American edition of *Past and Present* barely paid for itself. Carlyle's American readers merely waited a few weeks for the unauthorized cheap reprints, which they bought instead. Disgusted, Carlyle suggested to Emerson that they stop publishing each other's books, for English "pirates" had been stealing Emerson's royalties from the first series of *Essays* in the same manner. "Here too, you see, it is the same," he wrote in October of 1843. "Such chivalries therefore are now impossible; for myself I say, 'Well let them cease; thank God they once were, the memory of that can never cease with us!' " (L, p. 349). Although both men would violate it on occasion, their resolution had a good effect on their relationship. For one thing, it showed that each writer was so well known in the other's country that widespread piracy was inevitable. More important, it rescued their correspondence from a growing concern with business, trade, publishing firms: in short, with money. Carlyle was warmly touched by the pages crowded with figures and computations personally drawn up by Emerson beginning in 1839, but he may have wondered if his American friend was really a writer as he claimed or an accountant. In a few of his letters Carlyle seemed to be addressing him more as an agent than as a fellow author. After the failure of Emerson's *Past and Present,* "bibliopoly" never again threatened to usurp the main function of the correspondence: the meeting of two powerful minds.

Perhaps to compensate Carlyle for his lost royalties, Emerson composed an enthusiastic but thoughtful review of *Past and Present* for *The Dial.* As a "political tract," he proclaimed it comparable to the work of Milton and Burke, and he praised Carlyle for the creation of a "great connection, if not a system of thoughts" (EW 12:378). The article perceptively calls attention to the radical/reactionary schism in the book and shrewdly, though incorrectly, explains the contradictions as the effect of calculated satire. "Here is a book as full of treason as an egg is full of meat," the review jovially declares, "and every lordship and worship and high form and ceremony of English conservatism tossed like a football into the air, and kept in the air, with merciless kicks and rebounds, and yet not a word is punishable by statute." Carlyle protects himself from conservative censure by "impressing the reader with the conviction that the satirist himself has the truest love for everything old and excellent in English land and institutions" (pp. 384-385). Carlyle, of course, had no fear of censorship and disapproval; his political ambivalence arose from other, deeper sources. In fact, the terms of the contradiction Emerson ascribed to him have little to do with *Past and Present,* which he would hardly have considered treasonous. Nor did he really desire to kick the ruling classes up into the air; on the contrary, he kicked them in order to get them on their feet, with their feet on the ground, so that they might take command of society, as they should. Furthermore, he had little love for "everything old and excellent" merely for the sake of its antiquity; in *Past and Present* he referred to hoary institutions of the sort Emerson had in mind as "yellow parchments," venerable but in themselves practically worthless.

Emerson was really describing his own ambivalence toward England. He was concerned about England, and so he was disturbed by Carlyle's dour analysis of English social conditions, which he thought exaggerated (pp. 385-386). He observed that at least English culture was healthy, a point cagily supported at the end of the review by declaring Carlyle the most advanced expression of that culture: "the first domestication of the modern system . . . into style" (p. 390). But Emerson's concern for England was not mere sympathy. He was aware that he himself lived, in more ways than one, in a new England, and all his life he wondered to what extent, for better or worse, the new world would share or duplicate the fate of the old. In addition to a common language, culture, and ethnic origin, the two nations at that time had in common serious problems. As he wrote in the review, "We at this distance are not so far removed from any of the specific evils, and are deeply participant in too many, not to share the gloom" (pp. 387-388). Yet England and America differed in one respect which he considered all-important. They occupied different places on the earth.

His main criticism of *Past and Present* is best understood in light of his characteristic (though not unexceptionable) faith in geography, for in effect he accused Carlyle of being too historical. The objection appears in the review but was actually his immediate reaction, first expressed in a letter to Carlyle written just days after the arrival of the original Teufelsdröckhian bundle of printed sheets and crabbed manuscript. He told Carlyle that his only quarrel was "with the popular assumption . . . that the state of society is a new state, and was not the same thing in the days of Rabelais, & of Aristophanes, as of Carlyle" (L, p. 342). In the sense that society can always be saved by the eternal virtues of self-denial and hero worship, Carlyle would have assented; perhaps that understanding led him afterwards to affirm the correctness of the review (pp. 349-350), though he never replied directly to the letter. But Emerson meant what he said literally; society, he felt, is always the same, a premise which not only negates the entire concept of *Past and Present* (and makes the very title meaningless), but calls into question the value of historiography itself. If society is always the same, then historical judgments are arbitrary. He thought that Carlyle's assessment of the condition of England was not only too pessimistic but also largely subjective. As in the *Dial* review, only more succinctly, the letter attributes to "the historian" a tendency "to mix himself in some manner with his erring & grieving nations," which "so saddens the picture." (Carlyle, of course, regarded precisely those historians who did not mix themselves in as Dryasdusts.) He liked *Past and Present* as a "true contemporary history," as opposed, presumably, to a historical history; the *Dial* piece mentions Abbot Samson only once. Yet his antipathy toward history was ideological rather than temperamental. He really loved history; his biographer traces "an insatiable curiosity about history" to his boyhood.[31] One of his first courses of lectures was entitled "The Philosophy of History" (1836-37). Even so, in his maturity he came to regard history as dangerous, or at best suspect.

He gave history an important place in his writings, only to belittle its accomplishments and decry its failings. He selected "History" as the opening piece in his first series of *Essays,* but at the end of that essay he reviled "our so-called History" as "a shallow village tale" and an "old chronology of selfishness and pride" (EW 2:40). His first book, *Nature,* also opens with an attack on history:

> Our age is retrospective. It builds the sepulchres of the fathers. It writes biographies, histories, and criticism. The foregoing generations beheld God and nature face to face; we, through their eyes. Why should not we also enjoy an original relation to the universe? Why should not we have a poetry and philosophy of insight and not of tradition, and a religion by revelation to us, and not the history of theirs? (*NAL,* p. 7)

Instead of Carlyle's "Message, verbal or written, which all Mankind delivers to every man," history for Emerson was a veil or a shroud — an opaque, corpse's eyeball — that blocked out or distorted the message of nature. A preoccupation with the past is morbid, he came to feel. "A new day, a new harvest, new duties, new men, new fields of thought, new powers call you," he wrote in his journal in 1842, "and an eye fastened on the past unsuns nature, bereaves me of hope, & ruins me with a squalid indigence which nothing but death can adequately symbolize."[32] In the essay "Circles," he called himself "an endless seeker with no Past at my back," though he did not say what he was seeking or from what he was running.

His country could also claim to have no past at its back. "History has to live with what was here" — so begins the title poem in the collection *History* by Robert Lowell, another American both fascinated by the past and obsessed by the conjunction of history and death: "It is so dull and gruesome how we die." But what if "what was here" was nothing: would there then be history at all? In Emerson's "The Young American" (1844), America is called "a country of beginnings" and "the country of the Future." "It has no past: all has an onward and prospective look" (*NAL,* p. 230). Emerson wondered whether the American present were bound to the European past after all. And if so, were both worlds then destined for a common future? Or was the American Revolution temporal as well as political: were the two continents separated by time as well as by water? He had difficulty answering these questions because he was drawn in different directions at once: to the east and the west, to the past and the future, to England and America.

It would be tempting to explain his failure to appreciate the historical contrasts in *Past and Present,* as well as his suspicion that Carlyle's gloomy portrait of modern England was exaggerated, by suggesting that his life in a rural town in an agricultural country made it unlikely that he could conceive of the total, cataclysmic transformation of life in Britain through industrialization. As Walter E. Houghton points out, any Victorian would realize from "a mere glance at the title page" that Carlyle's book would compare the serene, simple Middle Ages with the chaotic, technological nineteenth century; the ages were considered as antithetical

as the very words, "past and present."[33] But while it is true
that Emerson, unlike Carlyle, had not observed the benefits
and evils of a paleotechnic economy first hand, and would
not have an opportunity to do so until his second visit to
England, nevertheless he was aware all along that something
unprecedented was occurring. Moreover, he prophesied as
early as 1837 that the same massive industrialization would
come soon to New England. Not only did he foresee it, but
he welcomed it in a tone that was, in Leo Marx's phrase,
"distinctly millennial."[34] The year 1837 was also the year of
"The American Scholar," in which he said that the best time
to be born is in an "age of Revolution; when the old and the
new stand side by side, and admit of being compared"
(*NAL*, p. 67). The context of the remark is a discussion of
literature, but, as everyone recognizes, the address concerns
more than scholarship. Not surprisingly, "The American
Scholar" was the first work by Emerson unreservedly admired by Carlyle.

In the early 1840s Emerson got a taste of the future right
in Concord. Work began on a railroad; miserably oppressed
Irish laborers were brought in, threatening to displace the
local peasants. A regular run to Boston began in June of
1844; the suburbanization of Concord began with it.[35] The
previous December he told Carlyle how he had moved to
Concord "because it was the quietest of farming towns," but
now "a railroad is a-building through our secretest wood-
lands." He found the "petty revolution" caused by the railroad "very odious to me when it began," but he added, re-
signedly, "it is hard to resist the joy of all one's neighbours,
and I must be contented to be carted like a chattel in the
cars & be glad to see the forest fall" (L, p. 355). Less than
two months later he delivered a lecture in Boston which presented an ecstatic vision of America's future industrial
greatness.

"The Young American" was one of those lectures he never
mentioned to Carlyle, preferring not to spoil his image as an
impractical dreamer. In fact, three weeks after the lecture

he was writing to him about the "happy hours" he had spent "gazing from afar at the splendours of the Intellectual Law." By now he was well aware of the effect such language had on Carlyle. "You sometimes charge me with I know not what sky-blue sky-void idealism," the letter goes on, and, in light of "The Young American," the charge is answered rather disingenuously: "I fear I may be more deeply infected than you think me. I have very joyful dreams which I cannot bring to paper, much less to any approach to practice" (pp. 358-359). Little did Carlyle know that his ineffectual American friend had spoken recently on such matters as: the swelling of Boston into the "metropolis of New England"; the annihilation of distance by roads, steamboats, and the "network of iron"; the exploitation of Irish immigrants; the irresistible growth of commercial power; and the contribution of American cooperative communities to the worldwide trend toward "beneficent socialism." The joyful dreams that he told Carlyle he could not bring to paper constitute, in the terminology of Leo Marx, sort of an industrial pastoral: "a railway journey in the direction of nature." Somehow America would become industrial yet remain agricultural, urban but still rural, both technological and natural—joyful dreams, indeed, but hardly the misty stuff Carlyle supposed Concord dreams were made of!

He did publish the lecture in *The Dial* but never called Carlyle's attention to it, and Carlyle, buried in Cromwelliana and concerned over the rapidly failing health of John Sterling, probably never read it. Emerson's reluctance may have arisen from reservations over his remarks in the lecture about England. The piece begins and ends with a denunciation of European (in particular English) "feudalism," which acts as a code word for everything he disliked about the old world, especially its rigid social hierarchies. His criticisms are vague and impressionistic, though Carlyle's influence occasionally sharpened the focus, as in the portrait of a "worthless lord" lording it over a "proud commoner," and in the lament for unwanted children, "threatening, starved weavers, and a pauperism now constituting one-thirteenth of the population" (*NAL,* p. 243). But he was not composing a jeremiad against England; he was delivering a message to Americans. And the message is that in order to achieve the industrial/pastoral utopia, America must dissociate herself from England completely and forever. American deference to European culture is an irreconcilable contradiction: "a false state of things," he called it near the start of the lecture, "newly in a way to be corrected. America is beginning to assert itself . . . and Europe is receding in the same degree" (p. 222). He handsomely allowed England its "many virtues, many advantages, and the proudest history in the world." But there is nothing suggestive of fellow feeling with the countrymen of his ancestors; in fact, the lecture ends with the sentiment that the problems of England have no bearing on America whatever. "It is for Englishmen to consider, not for us: we only say, let us live in America, too thankful for our want of feudal institutions." By leaving England, Americans have also left behind the past. Geography cancels history: "We shall quickly enough advance out of all hearing of other's censures, out of all regrets of our own, into a new and more excellent social state than history has yet recorded" (p. 244). The young American is free to seek the future with no past — with no England — at his back.

I do not mean to imply that Emerson was reluctant to antagonize Carlyle with the Anglophobic overtones in "The Young American." As we have seen, Carlyle had been delighted with a better known, though less extreme, early expression of Emerson's nationalism, "The American Scholar." A year before "The Young American" Emerson had touched on similar themes in a lecture course on "New England," and although he never published the series, he had outlined its contents for Carlyle in the same letter which conveyed his first reaction to *Past and Present* (L, p. 341). What happened, I think, is that he began to have second thoughts about his negative attitude toward England and to wonder if he really understood what was occurring in England at the present time. In 1840 he had assured Carlyle that "the view of Britain is excellent from New England" (p. 283), but as that eventful decade — Britain's "hungry forties" —wore on, he probably decided that he needed a closer look. A powerful catalyst in the formation of his resolution to revisit England was surely his reading of *Past and Present*. His immediate response had been to play down the gravity of the crisis Carlyle depicted, or to deny its existence entirely, attributing everything to the historian's subjectivity. But in the "Young American" lecture he alluded to the problems Carlyle had described as a genuine crisis, only to consign the British to their fate and absolve his countrymen of all concern. It is as though he was saying to Carlyle (or would have been saying had he asked Carlyle to read the lecture): perhaps your bitter forecast is accurate; still that is nothing to us, for we are not the same people.

But Carlyle and Emerson both felt that they *were* the same people. Carlyle in particular, for all his pejorative remarks about "Yankeeland," was continually reminding Emerson of their consanguinity. In his very first letter to Emerson, while "looking over the water" at his new friend, he took the opportunity to "repeat once more what I believe is already dimly the sentiment of all Englishmen, Cisoceanic and Transoceanic, that we and you are *not* two countries, and cannot for the life of us be; but only two *parishes* of one country." And what held the two countries together was more than voluntary friendship. "I am weary of hearing it said, 'We love the Americans,' 'we wish well' &c &c," Carlyle complained, "what in God's name should we do else?" (L, p. 102). Emerson answered Carlyle's "spiritual tokens of a fraternal friendliness" in kind (p. 106), though in later years, as he grew more nationalistic, he probably came to resent somewhat Carlyle's pan-Saxon assumptions. In a letter of 1838, for example, Carlyle asserted that "New England is becoming more than ever part of Old England" (p. 205), which of course was the very thing Emerson had been trying to combat the previous year in "The American

Scholar." The 1838 letter mentions another recurring theme between them, that London is the Anglo-Saxon capital; the "meeting of *All the English*" Carlyle called it in 1841 (p. 305). "London is properly *your* Mother City too," he wrote in 1847, after learning of Emerson's impending visit. The American should come and look and "say to this Land, 'Old Mother, how are you getting on at all?' To which the Mother will answer, 'Thankee, young son, and you?'—in a way useful to both parties" (p. 423). That was exactly what Emerson had in mind. "I shall come some fine day to see you in your burly city," he wrote a week before his departure, "you in the centre of the world, and sun me a little in your British heart" (p. 430). If they truly were the same people, then an American visiting the most advanced nation on earth would be confronting both the past and the future. Whatever was there, Emerson wanted very much to know; that was the main reason he undertook the British lecture tour that would finance the trip. "The main end answered here," he wrote his wife from Manchester, "is, faithful seeing of England."[36]

There was much to see, especially in London, where he passed almost all the spring of 1848, the final and most significant portion of his visit. Over the winter he had been committed to a grueling schedule of lectures in northern England and Scotland; now he was free for recuperation and exploration. "The most wonderful thing I see is this London at once seen to be the centre of the world," he wrote home in March, again employing the epithet he had used before his departure in the letter to Carlyle. Here he added another phrase:

the "nation in brick"; the immense masses of life of power of wealth, and the effect upon the men of running in & out amidst the play of this vast machinery, the effect to keep them tense & silent, and to mind every man his own, —it is all very entertaining, I assure you. I think sometimes that it would well become me to sit here a good while, and study London mainly, and the

wide variety of classes, that, like so many nations, are dwelling
here together. I have many good thoughts, many insights, as I
go up & down.[37]

An apocryphal story has Carlyle exhibiting the squalor of
London to Emerson in order to strengthen his belief in the
devil: a charming anecdote but not very likely, since view-
hunting in the slums would not have been in character for
either man. However, Carlyle did persuade Emerson to
attend a Chartist meeting, and Emerson was in London
when, in April, the Chartists' greatest demonstration was
suppressed by troops. Emerson, in other words, was able to
find things out on his own as he went up and down and met
a wide variety of classes, from the aristocrats who lionized
him to the self-educated workers who attended his less
expensive lecture courses. He was certainly not timid in seeking experience; Chartist meetings sometimes ended in violence. His quick trip to France in May was even more ad-
venturous. Tennyson warned him not to go and refused to
accompany him, but he was undaunted. For months he had
been hearing fearful talk from members of the upper classes
about the revolutionary wave on the Continent. Once again
the inspiration to take a firsthand look came from Carlyle,
who had been following the revolution in *The Times* and
was gratified to learn that Louis Philippe was getting what
he deserved. While in France, Emerson watched a street
scuffle (from a safe distance) and observed an assembly in
the Champ-de-Mars of over a million people. Early in June
he returned to London and almost immediately began a
new course of lectures "on the Mind and Manners of the
Nineteenth Century."[38] The surviving lecture notes suggest
that already he was applying to America what he had
learned about Europe, about England, and especially about
London. "Among the marks of the age of cities," he told his
audience, Carlyle among them, "must be reckoned conspicuously . . . the universal adoption of cash-payment." He
was no longer defiantly excluding America from the condi-

tion of England, as in "The Young American"; implicitly his remark encompasses America and Europe both. In a similar assertion a little further on — "in the universal expansion of the city by railroads, the stock-exchange infects our country-fairs" — an American (even a Concord) frame of reference is, I think, unmistakable.[39] By including America in "the age of cities," he was returning America to a place in history, as well as to a place in the family of Mother England.

But he still did not know what he thought of England, or, more important, what he thought of England and America. Several months passed after his return to Concord before he wrote to Carlyle in October of 1848. Only a fragment of a rough draft of the letter survives, but it is enough to illustrate his confusion as he described his response to people who asked about his trip:

> I made my best endeavour to praise the rich Country I had seen and its excellent energetic polished people. And it is very easy for me to do so. England is the country of success, & success has a great charm for me, more than for those I talk with at home. But they were obstinate to know if the English were superior to their possessions, and if the old religion warmed their hearts, & lifted a little the mountain of wealth. So I enumerated the list of brilliant persons I had seen, and the [gap in the text] But the question returned, Did you find kings & priests? Did you find sanctities & beauties that took away your memory, & sent you home a changed man, with new aims & with a discontent of your old pastures. (L, pp. 442-443)

The crude fragment is almost a miniature of *English Traits,* a book he would not complete until 1856. Both letter and book ask the same two questions, the second one tacitly. Are the English "superior to their possessions," or does the opulence of their possessions, which include their history and culture as well as material abundance, only mask their spiritual desolation and decline? And what effect, if any, should the condition of England have on Americans? The second question has unsettling ramifications. If the two countries are bound together, should Americans regard English greatness as a promise for their own future? And would English failures then constitute a warning? He could no longer entertain the alternative of "The Young American," that henceforward the two countries would go their separate ways; he had learned from his trip that the ties of race, history, and culture were too strong. He could hardly think about one country without thinking of the other. The first Carlyle heard of *English Traits* was in 1853 when Emerson wrote that he had "written hundreds of pages about England & America, & may send them to you in print" (p. 487). In 1843 Carlyle thought he saw what was wrong with England, and what had to be done to set it right, in a flash; he wrote *Past and Present* in a few weeks. Emerson struggled with England and America for eight years before he had something to send Carlyle in print. He had produced a book both fascinating in itself and of some historical significance, for *English Traits* was, in the words of a recent critic, Phyllis Cole, "the first substantial American study of a culture formed by modern technological power."[40] Yet the book fails to achieve the goals Emerson set for it.

The ostensible purpose of the book is revealed in the title: to delineate the characteristics of the English. The unstated purpose follows naturally: to speculate on how those characteristics function in a different geographical setting, specifically, of course, in America. "The American is only the continuation of the English genius into new conditions, more or less propitious" (*ET*, p. 22): that is the closest approach to a statement of the unstated goal. Emerson felt he was qualified for the job; he thought he knew both countries as well as one man possibly could. He knew the leaders of British culture personally, while he himself was a leader of American culture. He thought that "the view of Britain is excellent from New England" and probably expected to find the reverse equally true. He even would have considered himself prepared scientifically, for he was well read in the new and then highly regarded "science" of ethnology, or the study of race. He had been thinking about the racial traits of the English for many years; as early as 1835 he had delivered a lecture entitled "Permanent Traits of the English National Genius."[41] The goals of *English Traits* as I have described them are not breathtakingly ambitious, and surely they would not have seemed beyond his capability. After eight years of work on it, one might expect at the very least that he would come up with some hard and fast conclusions. But in place of conclusions *English Traits* offers a tangle of ambiguities. And the confusion, which I believe is partly contrived, not only emerges from the substance but extends to the very structure of the book.

It is impossible to determine his attitude toward England in general, let alone his conclusions. The best study of *English Traits*, Philip L. Nicoloff's *Emerson on Race and History*, argues persuasively, and from several directions, that the book is mainly pessimistic about the fate of the old world: "America was young, Europe was old, and historical necessity would take care of the rest."[42] However, in his introduction to the best edition of *English Traits*, Howard Mumford Jones professes astonishment at Nicoloff's idea "that Emerson was demonstrating the coming decadence of Great Britain. Is this not to read history backward?" According to Jones, "the extraordinary survival value of the English seems to be central in Emerson's estimate" (*ET*, p. xxi). As might be expected, the book supports both sides, at one point offering "the impression that the British power has culminated, is in solstice, or already declining" (p. 23), and elsewhere asserting that the British "have as much energy, as much continence of character as they ever had . . . and they exert the same commanding industry at this moment" (p. 69). To an extent Emerson was again using the dialectical method of *Representative Men*, here on a national scale, but with the essential difference that in *English Traits* there is no resolution at the end.

Although the critics cannot agree about his conclusions,

they are united in their dislike of his ending; both Jones and Nicoloff consider the "Speech at Manchester" superfluous and anticlimactic.[43] In some ways the occasion was more interesting than the speech it inspired. Shortly after his arrival in England Emerson addressed the annual banquet of the Manchester Athenaeum, which was attended by a "great and brilliant company," including the radical political leaders Richard Cobden, head of the Anti-Corn Law League, and John Bright, as well as men of wealth and title. (During the American Civil War the two radicals would both work as propagandists for the Union cause in England; according to Henry Adams, "Bright and Cobden were the hardest hitters" on his father's side.)[44] Emerson claimed to "have known all these persons already. When I was at home, they were as near to me as they are to you" (*ET*, p. 201). Aside from the people, he may also have been struck by the appropriateness of the setting. Here he was in Manchester, the center of British industry, speaking in a building called "Free-Trade Hall." Surely he must have recognized how symbolic it all was of what he had come to England to see.

Nicoloff regards the speech as "an example of gracious literary ambassadorship," tacked on to *English Traits* so "it would help soften some of the severe strictures of his earlier chapters."[45] I believe the intention was even more specific. Everyone who has taken a survey course in American literature should have heard how Emerson told Carlyle while they were traveling to Stonehenge for some sightseeing that "the geography of America" inspired a certain "feeling" in him: "that there and not here is the seat and centre of the British race; and that no skill or activity can long compete with the prodigious natural advantages of that country, in the hands of the same race; and that England, an old and exhausted island, must one day be contented, like other parents, to be strong only in her children" (*ET*, pp. 178-179). This powerful speech occurs at a dramatic moment in the book, for Emerson designed the "Stonehenge" chapter as the climax of *English Traits*. Now compare the end of the "Speech at Manchester," the closing words of the entire book:

I see her in her old age, not decrepit, but young and still daring to believe in her power of endurance and expansion. Seeing this, I say, All hail! mother of nations, mother of heroes, with strength still equal to the time . . . So be it! so let it be! If it be not so, if the courage of England goes with the chances of a commercial crisis, I will go back to the capes of Massachusetts and my own Indian stream, and say to my countrymen, the old race are all gone, and the elasticity and hope of mankind must henceforth remain on the Alleghany ranges, or nowhere. (p. 203)

They form a striking contrast, these two speeches, one spoken en route to an ancient Druid monument, the other in a hall dedicated to Free Trade, both in England. The forthright declaration of independence Emerson delivered to Carlyle held a personal meaning for the two old friends as well as a general message for the public. Carlyle always said that England and America were the same country, and London was the Saxon capital. Yes, we are the same people, Emerson acknowledged in "Stonehenge," and we are the same family, but the seat of the race has shifted westward: the center of the world is no more in London. England still is their old mother, but the children have grown and gone. At Manchester he also addressed England as a mother, but this time not necessarily as *his* mother. The awkward sentence replaced in my excerpt by an ellipsis may even hint at a denial of the relation: England, it says in part, is "only hospitable to the foreigner and truly a home to the thoughtful and generous who are born in the soil." But while retreating from the affirmation of consanguinity in "Stonehenge," the Manchester speech also in effect reverses the gloomy prophecy. England may be old, but she is not exhausted: "not decrepit, but young and still daring." The final sentence reflects the ambiguity created by the two speeches together. Perhaps England will fade after all; Emerson would then tell his "countrymen" that "the old race are all gone" but their spirit lives on in America. But everything in the sentence is tentative and vague, even grammatically ("If it be not so"), and nothing is resolved. He compounded the confusion — deliberately, I think — by using the "Speech at Manchester" as the conclusion of the book, which suggests finality. But he gave the speech at the very beginning of his visit, while the Stonehenge episode occurred almost at the very end, implying that the Stonehenge proclamation should be taken more seriously because it was based on a better acquaintance with England. However, he assembled the book many years after the visit; should not the final order, then, stand as his mature reconsideration? I feel the unsettled structure of the book consciously represents the author's own indecision.

To Emerson's credit, he ultimately rejected a facile resolution of his ambivalence along racial and class lines. Ever the dualist, he toyed with the idea of splitting the English into two camps: the "aristocratic," dilettante Normans of the upper class and the "democratic," practical Saxons of the middle and lower classes. He hedged his ethnological gambit by admitting that the distinction between "Norman" and "Saxon" was only metaphorical: "We are forced to use the names a little mythically, one to represent the worker and the other the enjoyer" (p. 48). Since America supposedly was settled by middle-class Saxons, the myth could support an assertion he had made earlier in the book which neatly divided the United States and Britain according to political temperament. In the chapter on "Race" he had compared the Atlantic Ocean to a "galvanic battery" separating antithetical substances. "So England tends to accumulate her liberals in America, and her conservatives in London" (p. 33). Such applications of "the hoary tale of Celt, Saxon, and Norman," as Nicoloff calls the racial theory Emerson appropriated,[46] would complement nicely the theme of the Stonehenge speech, that England was finished and the future belonged to progressive America. And the socio-racial demarcation (if social scientists will forgive my jargon) could just as easily justify the sentiment of Manchester — that England has life in her yet — by suggesting

that the vigorous, middle-class "Saxons" were replacing the
worn-out, upper-class "Normans" in England itself. He had
something of the sort in mind in the chapter on "Aristocracy." The logical conclusion would be that someday a
Saxon-dominated, middle-class England would come to
resemble middle-class, Saxon America, and in the chapter
on "The 'Times' " he indeed wrote that the "tendency in
England towards social and political institutions like those
of America is inevitable" (p. 170). And at the end of the
chapter on "Aristocracy" he had described the elevation of
the English middle class to a position of influence like that
of the American middle class.

He brought the idea of a Saxon-Norman dichotomy to
fruition in an important lecture called "The Anglo-American," which Phyllis Cole justly describes as "a final chapter
to *English Traits* not included in the published book."[47]
There he expanded the idea by bringing the Norman
character to America along with the Saxon and having the
lecturer speculate, in effect, about both countries:

> Which principle, which branch of the compound English
> race is here (+ now) to triumph? The liberty-loving, the
> thought-loving, the godly & grand British race, that have
> fought so many battles, + made so many songs, & created so
> many reverend laws & charters, & exhibited so much moral
> grandeur in private & poor men; — or, the England of Kings &
> lords; castles & primogeniture; enormous wealth & fierce ex-
> clusion? Which is to be planted here?[48]

These questions are answered later in the lecture with a di-
rectness all the more remarkable when compared to the indecision of *English Traits*. In a section of the manuscript
labeled "The Sturdy Minority," we are urged to

> remember the sturdy minority, often for an age majority, that,
> in England itself, has striven for the right, & the largest justice,
> & won so many charters, & still strives there with the lovers of
> liberty here. Rather it is right to esteem without regard to

geography this industrious liberty-loving Saxon wherever he
works, — the Saxon, the colossus who bestrides the narrow Atlantic, — at home in all seas. . . . Only let high & sound counsels
be given to these twin nations, admonishing, & holding them
up to their highest aim.[49]

Had he used "The Anglo-American" for the conclusion of
English Traits, he would have resolved the ambiguities of
that book in a manner pleasing to almost everyone in both
countries. Carlyle in particular would have been cheered to
hear his friend speak of "these twin nations," striving for
right and justice, bestriding the Atlantic, dominating the
world. But though he delivered the lecture often while he
was working on the book, he did not publish it. He never
mentioned it to Carlyle. And he left *English Traits* with its
built-in confusion intact.

His strain of nationalism accounts in part for the exclu-
sion of "The Anglo-American"; he did not want to commit
himself in print to a conception of England and America
"without regard to geography," or, as Carlyle had put it in
his letter of 1834, as "two parishes of one country." But
there was, I believe, a deeper reason. Despite his reading,
his traveling, and his experience with the coming of the railroad to Concord, when he sailed to England in 1847 Emerson could hardly have been prepared to face the first technological society. The England of the past, which he knew
from books and had toured as a young man, was still there,
but alongside it — in Manchester, in Birmingham, in
London — there was a new England, an England of the
future.[50] The direct references to industrialization in *English Traits* are curiously detached, even humorous, in tone,
but their lightness betrays their uneasiness. "Steam is almost
an Englishman," he wrote in the chapter, "Ability." "I do
not know but they will send him to Parliament next, to
make laws." The jokes have an anxious edge. "Gas-burners
are cheaper than daylight in numberless floors in the cities."
"Man is made as a Birmingham button" (*ET,* pp. 62-63). In

an early chapter on "Land," he sandwiched between paragraphs about geography, natural resources, and climate
these disturbing observations:

> The only drawback on this industrial conveniency is the
> darkness of its sky. The night and day are too nearly of a color.
> It strains the eyes to read and to write. Add the coal smoke. In
> the manufacturing towns, the fine soot or *blacks* darken the
> day, give white sheep the color of black sheep, discolor the
> human saliva, contaminate the air, poison many plants and
> corrode the monuments and buildings. (p. 24)

Supposedly he was merely recording what he saw, but the
words, in the short sentences and the vivid images, convey a
sense of dread. The chapter on "Wealth" describes the
dangers of steam, which "was dreadful with its explosion,
and crushed the engineer," and relates it to the far greater
dangers of "the dragon Money." He already knew about
depressions, for America had suffered more than one in his
lifetime. But he discovered that even in "the culmination of
national prosperity," in an advanced industrial country like
Britain, "it was found that bread rose to famine prices," the
"yeomen" lost their small farms, "and the dreadful barom-
eter of the poor-rates was touching the point of ruin" (pp.
108-109).

Perhaps the English would overcome the threat of technological dehumanization, as well as the more pressing evils
resulting from modern industry and commerce. But how
could he tell? Such a metamorphosis in the human condition had never happened before; it was all beyond his own
experience and beyond the collective experience of history.
"The machinery has proved, like the balloon, unmanageable, and flies away with the aeronaut" (p. 108). And in the
1850s, when he was assembling *English Traits*, he saw the
same forces at work in America. The new age had transformed the old England; now it was coming to New England. The strange clouds gathering at the horizon, soot-

darkened but glowing with power, were so unknowable that Emerson may have decided that it made little difference whether America faced the future alone, with no past at her back, or together with the mother country, England.

With regard to politics, the argument between Carlyle and Emerson centered on two issues: democracy and slavery. But though they stood on opposite sides in these matters, the philosophical premises underlying their attitudes are not far apart. Emerson's support of democracy, in fact, was no less qualified than Carlyle's opposition to it, at least in so far as the definition of "democracy" is limited to elected government. In "The Young American" Emerson spoke with Carlylean sarcasm of "our pitiful and most unworthy politics, which stake every gravest national question on the silly die, whether James or whether Jonathan shall sit in the chair and hold the purse" (*NAL*, p. 241). His general opinion of American democracy, as expressed in his essay on "Politics," was that its success was accidental, the result of conditions peculiar to a particular place and time. "Democracy is better for us, because the religious sentiment of the present time accords better with it" (EW 3:207). Similarly, in *Chartism* Carlyle acknowledged that democracy may "subsist" in America, at least temporarily, because so little government is needed there anyway, "save that of the parish-constable" (CW 29:158). But democracy meant more to Emerson than the ballot box.

"Society is a wave," he wrote in "Self-Reliance," meaning that the members of society really have as little to do with its nature as the water particles have to do with the wave. "The persons who make up a nation to-day, next year die, and their experience dies with them" (EW 2:87). Rulers may come to power through succession, election, or revolution; society is little affected because it proceeds under a different authority. "Nature is not democratic, nor limited-monarchical, but despotic," he explained in "Politics," "and will not be fooled or abated of any jot of her authority by the pertest of her sons" (EW 3:200). In politics, as in everything else, he felt it was advisable to cooperate with nature and essential not to oppose nature. Democracy is letting nature take its course.

But in advocating a government in cooperation with nature, he came up against the same obstacle that blocked Carlyle in his quest for a government of heroes: there is no way to find the right governors. Carlyle wanted leadership according to the will of the hero; for Emerson it was (in "Politics") "the will of the wise man," who of course was wise precisely in that he understood the higher sources of wisdom and power. But when society "makes awkward but earnest efforts to secure his government by contrivance" — and several "contrivances" are listed, among them voting — it is discovered that the wise man cannot be found by such mechanical means. The analysis thus far is similar to Carlyle's; the solution is very different. "Hence the less government we have the better — the fewer laws, and the less confided power" (EW 3:213-215). Government should "leave the individual . . . to the rewards and penalties of his own constitution" (p. 219). Government must not discourage individuality; everyone must be free to fulfill his nature. But while he wanted the government to leave the individual alone, he did not assent to laissez-faire; nor did he ever seriously entertain a theory of anarchism, though he sometimes seemed headed in that direction as well. Order and class are inevitable.

There are permanent hierarchies in society, he believed, just as in nature, and though he did not entirely agree with Carlyle that might makes right, he did not deny that the strong get their way. A revolution may unseat those in power, but, as he explained in the essay "Manners," "At once a new class finds itself at the top, as certainly as cream rises in a bowl of milk: and if the people should destroy class after class, until two men only were left, one of these would be the leader" (EW 3:129). There was a certain authoritarian tendency in Emerson. Although it did not become

prominent until the Civil War, when his bellicosity led him
to support an enlarged central government,[51] a longing for
strong leadership was sometimes apparent in earlier years.
In "The Young American," for example, he described "the
main duties of government" as "the duty to instruct the ignorant, to supply the poor with work and with good guidance" (*NAL*, p. 235). Carlyle, initially at least, did not ask
for more.

The difference between Emerson's authoritarianism and
Carlyle's can be seen in the well-known passage on "hypocritical prating about the masses" in Emerson's last major
work, *The Conduct of Life* (1860). In ironic anticipation, as
it were, of Carlyle's "Shooting Niagara" seven years later,
Emerson found work for the drill master among the American people, but with a different purpose in mind. He
wanted to take "the masses" and "to tame, drill, divide and
break them up, and draw individuals out of them" (EW
6:249). Emersonian drill would produce persons, not mech-
anized regiments. A regimented society was the last thing he
wanted.

There is a curious sentence in *English Traits*—"so syntac-
tically tangled" that Howard Mumford Jones was forced to
"read it two or three times"—which echoes Carlyle's totalitarian nightmare of the future. Emerson, of course, had
read the *Latter-Day Pamphlets*, with their call for industrial
regiments, long before he completed *English Traits*; he had
also discussed the projected series with Carlyle before he left
England.[52] In *English Traits* he ended the chapter on "Ability" with this reflection on the British:

> Whilst they are some ages ahead of the rest of the world in
> the art of living; whilst in some directions they do not represent
> the modern spirit but constitute it;—this vanguard of civility
> and power they coldly hold, marching in phalanx, lockstep,
> foot after foot, file after file of heroes, ten thousand deep. (*ET*,
> p. 65)

Swayed, perhaps, by the somewhat problematic word "heroes," Jones interprets this odd bit of writing as Emerson's expression of "the admirable outcome of the racial history" of the British as he had been tracing it in his book (p. xxi). Emerson may have admired the trend toward regimentation both as a manifestation of "the modern spirit" and as the realization of unprecedented power ("success has a great charm for me" he wrote Carlyle), but a man who wanted forcibly to break up the masses into individuals could hardly admire an image of social organization which reads like a description of a rally at Nuremberg. Instead of pure admiration, I believe the sentence reflects at least some of the same anxiety perceptible in his scattered comments on technology, and for much the same reason. There had never been large-scale industry before, so there had never been industrial armies, and he had no idea what they might portend.

In their own way, Emerson's social ideas are as ambivalent as Carlyle's. Daniel Aaron took from Emerson the title of his book about the American Progressives, *Men of Good Hope*, and he addressed the opening chapter to Emerson. Yet Aaron speaks of him as "synchronizing the predatory practices of the entrepreneur with the harmony of the universe" and sanctioning "unconsciously the forces of exploitation that were at work in the United States and the powerful men . . . who were directing this exploitation."[53] The reason for the apparent contradiction lies, I think, in Emerson's belief in amelioration, which was actually his doctrine of evolution. Like Tennyson in England, he anticipated certain evolutionary principles long before Darwin, though of course with great differences.[54] "Remark the unceasing effort throughout nature at somewhat better than the actual creatures," he wrote in "The Young American": *"amelioration in nature*, which alone permits and authorizes amelioration in mankind" (*NAL*, pp. 230-231). In the same way society advances to higher forms, and even the "predatory practices of the entrepreneur" become a force for the better, regardless of the entrepreneur's intentions:

> Trade is an instrument in the hands of that friendly Power which works for us in our own despite. We design it thus and thus; but it turns out otherwise and far better. This beneficent tendency, omnipotent without violence, exists and works. Every line of history inspires a confidence that we shall not go far wrong; that things mend. That is it. That is the moral of all we learn, that it warrants Hope, HOPE, the prolific mother of reforms. (p. 243)

Here is another reason for Emerson's disregard for history: all history can teach is that things will improve. He may have had doubts and questions about the future, but he clung to his belief in amelioration, even in later years, perhaps out of the conviction that we may as well hope for the best, since there is so little we can do about the future anyway.

His trust in amelioration was of the utmost importance in his life because it led him to oppose slavery. At first his opinions rather resembled those of Carlyle. Examine such early writings as the speech he delivered at Concord in 1837 (printed in Cabot's *Memoir*), the conclusion of a lecture given during the winter of the following year and later published as "The Tragic" (EW 12:415-417), and these lines from the "Ode Inscribed to W.H. Channing":

> The over-god
> Who marries Right to Might
> Who peoples, unpeoples,
> He who exterminates
> Races by stronger races
> Black by white faces,
> Knows to bring honey
> Out of the lion.

Evidently he believed, in the years before his address on "Emancipation in the British West Indies" (1844), that black people somehow were well suited for slavery, either because of moral failings or evolutionary retardation, that emancipation would bring more harm than good, and that in any event the slaves themselves did not mind their situation as much as the obnoxious humanitarians did. Like Carlyle, he felt that cannibalism characterized the human condition in the absence of civilization, as was supposedly the case among blacks.[55] Coincidentally, the immediate situation that turned him against slavery may have confirmed Carlyle in his support. Emerson decided that the freed blacks in the West Indies had indeed improved themselves, which convinced him that the ameliorative principle applied to all races. From that time on, he became an ever more fervid and active proponent of abolition.[56] Carlyle's conviction that emancipation had failed in the West Indies prompted him to write what is surely the most racist tract in English literature, the "Occasional Discourse on the Nigger Question" (1849).

The only plea that can be made on Carlyle's behalf regarding his sentiments on black slavery is that he was totally ignorant about the realities of slavery and too pig-headed to bother finding out the truth. John Sterling, it will be recalled, whose experiences on a plantation in the West Indies had turned him against slavery, tried to talk to him, but Carlyle would not really listen, and after Sterling's death there was hardly anyone with whom he would discuss the matter at all. John Stuart Mill, once a close friend of Carlyle, answered the "Nigger Question" with an angry letter to *Fraser's*, who had published it, but Carlyle and Mill long ago had stopped seeing each other.[57] In America, many people were incensed by the "Nigger Question" and by a stupid anti-American remark in the *Latter-Day Pamphlets* (cf. L, pp. 44-45). Carlyle's popularity began to decline in the North and to rise proportionately in the South, aided by

admirers like George Fitzhugh. Emerson refused to denounce his friend, but his loyalty must have been strained
and reluctant. At least during the Civil War Carlyle had
sense enough not to involve himself directly in the Confederate cause, despite the efforts of various importunate
Southerners who visited him in Chelsea.[58] But his sympathies were obvious to everyone.

In 1864 Emerson sent Carlyle a letter, his first in two
years, regretting his allegiance in "the battle for Humanity"
and wishing they had been on the same side. "Ah! how
gladly I would enlist you with your thunderbolt, on our
part!" And he was sorry that Carlyle had never come to
America as "in earlier years you projected or favored. It
would have made it impossible that your name should be
cited for one moment on the side of the enemies of mankind" (L, p. 541). Carlyle may have been surprised to learn
that Emerson opposed the slave states so fervently, even
though he had read (and, oddly, expressed approval of) the
West Indies speech years earlier (p. 367). Emerson was not
generally known in England to have been an abolitionist
until after his death, and he seldom spoke of slavery in his
letters to Carlyle (cf. pp. 499, 501-502).[59] Neither man ever
mentioned the "Nigger Question" article (at least not by
name). Presumably the topic did not come in for serious discussion during Emerson's visit, although he knew of Carlyle's position (cf. p. 38). But in any event, Carlyle was
deeply affected by the belated rebuke, or so contended
Moncure Conway, an anti-Confederate Virginian who saw
him frequently during the war. Conway claimed that Emerson's letter, along with a photograph he had seen a year earlier of a slave who had been flogged, almost brought Carlyle
to the point of recantation and repentance.[60]

But if his attitude softened as a result of Emerson's letter,
then it hardened again quickly, for a few years later he
became active in the defense of Edward John Eyre, who had
been widely censured for his brutal suppression of a black
rebellion in Jamaica in 1865, when he was governor. The

author of a recent article on the Eyre controversy feels that
Carlyle's support was not motivated by racism but was
"rather an expression of approval for a man who had not
been afraid to use his power as ruler."[61] That sounds plausible. But it is ironic, and perhaps symbolic, that both Carlyle
and Emerson defended men who were under fire for un-
popular causes: Carlyle championed Governor Eyre, while a
decade earlier Emerson had defended John Brown. It might
even be said that they supported such dissimilar men for
similar reasons, since Brown and Eyre were men of action of
the sort often admired by hero worshippers in their studies.
Yet regardless of their supporters' motivation, there can be
little doubt about the judgment of history on the man who
quelled the rebellion in Jamaica and the man who tried to
spark a revolt at Harpers Ferry.

History may not forgive Carlyle for the comfort he gave to
slave drivers and racists, in his own time and after, but his
friend did forgive him. He went even further. "Every reading person in America holds you in exceptional regard, &
will rejoice in your arrival," he wrote in 1870, begging
Carlyle yet again to visit the United States, for the people
"have forgotten your scarlet sins before or during the war."
Emerson himself had "long ceased to apologise for or
explain your savage sayings," because genius is "a large
infusion of Deity, & so brings a prerogative all its own" to
say whatever it wants. His list of such "anointed men" who
may be "laws to themselves" is illuminating, as well as
touching in view of the past:

> We must not suggest to Michel Angelo, or Machiavel, or
> Rabelais, or Voltaire, or John Brown of Ossawottomie, (a great
> man,) or Carlyle, how they shall suppress their paradoxes &
> check their huge gait to keep accurate step with the procession
> of the street sidewalk. They are privileged persons, & may have
> their own swing for me. (L, p. 575)

According to the Emersonian philosophy, Carlyle was no
more culpable for his lapse from greatness than John Brown

was responsible for his elevation to greatness; both were no more than conduits for large infusions of Deity. Had Carlyle ever visited America, even at the height of the Civil War, he probably would have been welcome nowhere more warmly than in Concord.

Carlyle was very pleased with *English Traits*; he thought it "worth all the Books ever written by New England upon Old" (a distinction for which it might still compete). The chapter on "Literature" confused him, but he did not say why. In that chapter he had been described as a man "driven by his disgust at the pettiness and the cant, into the preaching of Fate" (*ET*, p. 161).[62] His letter ends plaintively: "Oh my friend, save always for me some corner in y^r memory: I am very lonely in these months and years" (L, pp. 517-518). Eight years earlier, when the two men were alone at Stonehenge, he had spoken out of a similar sense of loneliness and self-pity. Emerson remembered in *English Traits*:

> We walked in and out and took again a fresh look at the uncanny stones. The old sphinx put our petty differences of nationality out of sight. To these conscious stones we two pilgrims were alike known and near. We could equally well revere their old British meaning. My philosopher was subdued and gentle. In this quiet house of destiny he happened to say, "I plant cypresses wherever I go, and if I am in search of pain, I cannot go wrong." (*ET*, p. 181)

Their petty national differences returned to sight a couple of days later, on a rainy Sunday that afforded an opportunity for "much discourse." Emerson was challenged by Carlyle and some other Britons to produce "an American idea, — any theory of the right future of that country." Before answering, Emerson ruled out in his mind anything that merely "would make of America another Europe." Finally he said that there *was* an American idea, "but those who hold it are fanatics of a dream which I should hardly care to relate to your English ears, to which it might be only ridiculous, — and yet it is the only true." Anticipating "the objections and the fun," he then went on to talk about "no-government and non-resistance," and making revolutions without guns but through "love and justice alone." He "fancied that one or two of my anecdotes made some impression on Carlyle," because he sounded so saintly that "when dinner was announced, Carlyle refused to go in before me, — 'he was altogether too wicked' " (pp. 185-186).[63] The gentle mood they had enjoyed at Stonehenge made their differences seem insignificant, and the tranquil afterglow enabled them to have a little fun with the political and national issues both took so seriously. But the Stonehenge spirit could not last forever, except in some corner of memory.

Conclusion

Emerson traveled all over the country delivering lectures until he was well into his sixties. On one occasion in 1866 he was stranded by a snowstorm in Davenport, Iowa, and he rewarded the people who put him up for the night with several hours of conversation, including some amusing anecdotes about Carlyle. His host particularly enjoyed a story about a wealthy American who, when he told Carlyle how much he admired him and how much trouble he had taken to meet him, found that Carlyle simply refused to believe a word he said. The Iowan recalled that Emerson "fairly laughed aloud" at the eccentric manner of his friend, for whom he offered no apology.[1] It was a happy time for Emerson, and his most readable letters to Carlyle, describing his wanderings and adventures, were written during those last years.[2]

Carlyle's last letters to Emerson were, on the whole, much less cheerful. In 1866 his wife died suddenly, and he never overcame the shock. Almost a year later he described himself in a letter to Emerson as "a gloomily serious, silent and sad old man," and he seemed to be wishing his own death (L, p. 551). Emerson could also at times strike a somber note, for he, too, was feeling the approach of death. "To live too long is the capital misfortune," he wrote Carlyle in 1864—in the very same letter, in fact, in which he blasted Carlyle's position on the Civil War.[3] No doubt with these two passages in mind, an early reviewer of the Carlyle-Emerson correspondence remarked, "It is very melancholy to find the two old men, with all their boasted transcendental faith," indulging in such morbid animadversions.[4] But the truth is that to the very last both writers preserved something of the upbeat, forward-looking quality with which their correspondence began. "Alas, alas here is the end of the paper, dear Emerson," wrote Carlyle at the close of his final letter, "and I had still a whole wilderness of things to say. Write to me, or even do not write, *and* I will surely write again" (L, p. 589). He never did write again, but a few months later, in October of 1872, Emerson set sail for England, and the two old friends were together once more.

Emerson undertook his third trip abroad for the same reason as the first: to recover from a personal crisis. In 1832 it had been the loss of his first wife; this time it was the destruction of his Concord home in a fire. Accompanied by his daughter Ellen, he toured the Continent and the Near East, then stopped again in England before returning to America and a rebuilt house. He did not spend a great deal of time with Carlyle, and what little there was could not have been very productive, since they were both rather advanced in their senility. Emerson had been suffering from loss of memory and difficulty in speaking for years; during his final stay in London he amused his daughter by suggesting that they take an obelisk (instead of an omnibus—surely an aphasic complication of excessive view-hunting in Egypt).[5] Carlyle may have been less impressed with Emerson than with Ellen, who seems to have uttered opinions on racial matters agreeable to the author of the "Nigger Question." But Carlyle's brain was also clouded by age. On the afternoon he meant to see Emerson off, he wasted time fiddling with a clogged pipe, then walked part of the way with a friend, decided it was too late and went back home. Emerson probably had left London the day before anyway (L, pp. 57-58).

During their last years they exchanged gifts and heard indirect reports on each other from mutual acquaintances. The year before he died, Carlyle asked Moncure Conway to send Emerson his love and added: "I still think of his visit to us at Craigenputtock as the most beautiful thing in our experience there." But his friend's mind was all but gone; Norton wrote in a letter to Carlyle that Emerson had been reminiscing about a visit from Carlyle in Concord (which of course never occurred). On the day Carlyle was buried in Scotland, Emerson somehow managed to read a paper at a memorial gathering in Boston. A few weeks before his own death he pointed to a picture of Carlyle and said, "That is my man, my good man!" (L, pp. 61-63). They both died peacefully.

The publication of Charles Eliot Norton's edition of the Carlyle-Emerson correspondence in 1883 prompted a reevaluation of their relationship, especially in Britain, where the tendency to regard Emerson as Carlyle's protege lingered despite Emerson's immense popularity.[6] In America, on the other hand, Emerson had neither master nor rival; long forgotten were the early attempts to dismiss him as Carlyle's acolyte in the latest form of infidelity. Americans were more sensitive to the differences between the two and more likely to assert Emerson's independence than were the British: thus Lowell's versified *Fable for Critics* (1848) ridiculed those "persons, mole-blind to the soul's make and style, / Who insist on a likeness 'twixt him and Carlyle."[7] It is possible that the *Correspondence* had the opposite effect on the opposing sides of the Atlantic, reuniting the two names in the United States and distinguishing them in Britain. Americans were reminded of the importance of their friendship, particularly for Emerson in the early years; and the British learned that, as Carlyle once wrote to Emerson, the reciprocity was not all on one side. The "early devotion of the disciple to his master," wrote a critic of the *Correspondence* in the *Fortnightly Review*, "lapsed gracefully into a more equal relation."[8]

One Englishman of great stature, Matthew Arnold, went so far as to suggest that Carlyle might be remembered more for his letters to Emerson than for anything else he ever wrote.[9] Arnold's discourse on Emerson, which remains the best known evaluation of Emerson and Carlyle, is most remarkable for its willful lack of objectivity, although Arnold, it goes without saying, valued objectivity highly. He tried to disguise his bias through a pose of cautious moderation. "I cannot think that what I have said of Emerson will finally be accounted scant praise," he wrote of the speech later, implying that he had weighted his opinions so delicately that the tilt of the balance in Emerson's favor will be perceptible ("finally") only at some future date.[10] And it is true that he had described Emerson as a mediocre poet and philosopher and not a "great writer." Nevertheless, in the discourse he flatly called Emerson's *Essays* "the most important work done in prose" in the century, comparable to Wordsworth's poetry. And he immediately, and rather gratuitously, added: "His work is more important than Carlyle's. Let us be just to Carlyle, provoking though he often is."[11] The latter sentence gives the game away; Arnold would be "just" to Carlyle only to lend legitimacy to his assassination.

As I said, Arnold was willing to permit Carlyle's name to live as the coauthor of the *Correspondence*, but he slammed shut the door on any other hope for a literary afterlife. "Emerson freely promises to Carlyle immortality for his histories," he observed. But Arnold bluntly revoked the promise: "They will not have it. Why?" Arnold's answer so begs the question that it amounts to an unconscious self-parody: "Because the materials furnished to him . . . were not wrought in and subdued by him to what his work, regarded as a composition for literary purposes, required."[12] The essay almost leaves the impression that Arnold's sole purpose in praising Emerson was to use him as a whetstone (rather than a touchstone) to grind the axe intended for Carlyle.

Yet Arnold's preference for Emerson was longstanding. "Emerson has always particularly interested me by retaining his reason," he wrote to Moncure Conway in 1865, "while Carlyle, his fellow prophet, lost his."[13] It is difficult to determine when Arnold's early admiration for Carlyle changed to antipathy. For that matter, it is virtually impossible to understand his complex attitude toward Carlyle at all; he probably did not understand it himself. "Again and again in Arnold," observes David J. DeLaura in his indispensable article on the subject, "we come upon a peculiar psychological mechanism whereby Carlyle will be rejected with expressions of scorn, distrust, or condescension, while the surrounding text will, in a variety of ways, reveal its substantive debt to Carlyle's writings."[14] DeLaura shows how Arnold sometimes incorporated Carlyle's ideas and his language (including the key Arnoldean term "Philistine") without acknowledgment and perhaps even without awareness.

In the Emerson speech Arnold damns Carlyle for his "perverse attitude towards happiness." He predictably misreads Teufelsdröckh's rhetorical question—"What if thou wert born and predestined not to be Happy, but to be Unhappy!"—as a positive endorsement of misery. It was a familiar accusation, and Carlyle was certainly vulnerable on such grounds. What is surprising is the confused and ineffectual manner in which Arnold prosecutes the attack. Just "the other day," he says, he read a bizarre little tract which condemned smoking because it is enjoyable and (Arnold quotes the tract) an " 'earnest man will expressly avoid what gives agreeable sensations.' " The implication is that Carlyle, like the earnest author of the tract, did not want people to enjoy themselves at all. The illustration is not only silly, it is also peculiarly inapposite. Arnold practically calls attention to its inappropriateness himself when he adds: "I do not happen to be a smoker myself"; for it was well known that smoking was Carlyle's favorite petty vice. Arnold quickly recovers with a school inspection anecdote which enables him to berate Carlyle's pessimism in a more telling manner and finally to dismiss him for good. That clears the stage for the apotheosis of Emerson, which closes the piece. For Arnold has heard "Emerson's gospel" of "happiness and

eternal hope," and so in his mind's eye Emerson remateri-
alizes "in his habit as he lived, but of heightened stature and
shining feature," with his arms stretched out to east and
west.[15]

Arnold's attitude toward Carlyle and Emerson should be
examined alongside the scattered but brilliant comments of
Nietzsche. Like Arnold, Nietzsche unequivocally preferred
Emerson to Carlyle. And as with Arnold, certain of Nietzsche's ideas bear some resemblance to certain ideas of
Carlyle, and (again like Arnold) Nietzsche never called attention to the similarities.[16] (However, there is no question
with Nietzsche of unattributed borrowings.) Yet in a few
brief paragraphs and detached phrases, Nietzsche demonstrated that his perception of the two writers, and especially
of Carlyle, was more profound than the pronouncements of
Arnold (or of just about anyone else).

According to Nietzsche, Carlyle was the victim of a "psychological confusion": specifically, "the demand for belief
— confused with the 'will to truth.' "[17] Thus in *The Antichrist* he describes "Carlylism, if one will forgive me this
word," as "the need for faith, for some kind of unconditional Yes and No."[18] He develops this provocative analysis
in miniature to the fullest extent in the segment of *Twilight
of the Idols* called "Skirmishes of an Untimely Man," in
which sections 12 and 13 are devoted to Carlyle and Emerson respectively.[19] Carlyle is accused of a "constant passionate dishonesty against himself," though it is for that very
reason that "he is and remains interesting." Nietzsche concludes that in reality Carlyle was an "atheist who makes it a
point of honor not to be one." In contrast, Emerson was
"more enlightened, more roving, more manifold, subtler
than Carlyle; above all, happier." Even so, he refers to a
sentiment that Carlyle ("who loved him very much") expressed shortly after Emerson's arrival in London in 1847, to
the effect that Emerson does not offer enough to chew on.[20]
The criticism, Nietzsche concedes, "may be true, but is no
reflection on Emerson" because he "has that gracious and

clever cheerfulness which discourages all seriousness." He concludes the "skirmish" with some shrewd remarks on Emerson's ability to maintain a boyish disposition despite old age; in a curiously apt comparison, he suggests that Emerson has the "cheerful transcendency" of an elderly gentleman who returns from an assignation so pleased with his lustful appetite that he accepts with equanimity his inability to satisfy it.

Nietzsche's opinion of Carlyle and Emerson is not very different from Arnold's, but Nietzsche expresses it much more directly and reveals a great depth of insight into the nature of the two men. Carlyle's characteristic gloom is not a symptom of perversity but the product of a fundamental confusion of faith and truth. Emerson's happiness is so infectious because he more than compensates for a lack of substance with a "clever cheerfulness which discourages all seriousness." Nietzsche would have agreed, I think, with the observation of Henry James, cited in my Introduction, that both of them were a little mad, only in different ways.

Like Arnold, Nietzsche derived great joy from Emerson; only he did not find it necessary to declare his gratitude by issuing grandiose statements about his work or by invoking a resurrected Emerson standing with outstretched arms, shining and larger than life. Borrowing an image from Nietzsche, the author of a little book on his relation to Emerson eloquently sums up Nietzsche's attitude by likening him to a wanderer who listens appreciatively to a birdsong without, of course, understanding it. "Thus Nietzsche paused near Emerson, enchanted by the thrush's voice, only to set out on the road again with renewed strength, at the same time freshly aware of his loneliness."[21]

But a question remains: why were both Arnold and Nietzsche so determined to reject Carlyle and embrace Emerson? To seek an answer, it is necessary to leave Arnold and Nietzsche and return once more to Carlyle and Emerson.

Emerson may have been aware of the "psychological confusion" which Nietzsche diagnosed in Carlyle: the inability

—or the unwillingness—to separate the demand for belief from the will to truth. "I had a good talk with C[arlyle] last night," he wrote in his notebook "England" in October of 1847:

> He says over & over, for months, for years, the same thing. Yet his guiding genius is his moral sense, his perception of the sole importance of truth & justice; and he, too, says that there is properly no religion in England.[22]

When this passage was adapted for Emerson's memorial speech on Carlyle in 1881, Emerson (or someone) added that Carlyle's truth was a "truth of character, not of catechisms" (EW 10:495). Perhaps Emerson came to realize that it was Carlyle's misfortune to be dissatisfied with truth of character alone; he wanted catechisms as well, but catechisms that were true.

Emerson felt that everyone shared the demand for belief which Nietzsche observed in Carlyle. In one of the finest of his *Essays,* "Experience," he wrote: "It is not what we believe concerning the immortality of the soul or the like but *the universal impulse to believe,* that is . . . the principal fact in the history of the globe" (EW 3:74). Part of Emerson's secret, I feel, is that he could accept the demand for belief as a form of belief in itself. He was fascinated by the very falsehood of belief and by the illusory nature of truth. "Dream delivers us to dream," he wrote in "Experience," "and there is no end to illusion" (p. 50). Here is the hazy, mountaintop Emerson who so exasperated Carlyle, partly because he envied his equilibrium. As Nietzsche remarked, Carlyle needed an "unconditional Yes and No"; Emerson acquiesced in uncertainty.

After their season of Transcendental youth, they grew apart in many ways, but in the autumn of their lives the hidden congruity of their minds began to draw them back together. Carlyle read *The Conduct of Life,* Emerson's last important book, and in my opinion his best, with more sympathy and admiration than he had ever expressed for any of his friend's works. "You have grown older, more pungent, piercing," he wrote; "I never read from you before such lightning-gleams of meaning as are to be found here" (L, pp. 533-534). It was not that Emerson had extended or clarified his thinking, much less changed any of his ideas. Instead, as Carlyle remarked, his manner of expression had ripened; he had become sharper, less milky, more potent. Carlyle especially liked the final essay, "Illusions."

In "Illusions" Emerson resumed the theme he had taken up in "Experience" and elsewhere, that belief is illusory by nature and yet the demand for belief is a universal trait. He rarely discarded an idea, and echoes of his thought and learning from many periods of his life may be found in "Illusions." For instance, the Kantian conception of space and time "as simply forms of thought" — one of the principal ghosts of Transcendentalism — haunts the essay (EW 6:320). But here the old, fleeting ideas are pursued with relentless determination:

> The chapter of fascinations is very long. Great is paint; nay, God is the painter; and we rightly accuse the critic who destroys too many illusions . . . I find men victims of illusion in all parts of life. Children, youths, adults and old men, all are led by one bawble or another . . . All is riddle, and the key to a riddle is another riddle. There are as many pillows of illusion as flakes in a snow-storm. We wake from one dream into another dream. (p. 313)

At one point the tone modulates still further, almost to the key of despair:

> Like sick men in hospitals, we change only from bed to bed, from one folly to another; and it cannot signify much what becomes of such castaways, wailing, stupid, comatose creatures, lifted from bed to bed, from the nothing of life to the nothing of death. (p. 322)

It is the same bleak truth that Carlyle's Transcendentalism foundered upon in "Natural Supernaturalism": "We emerge from the Inane; haste stormfully across the astonished Earth; then plunge again into the Inane." Emerson has joined Carlyle in facing the desolation and admitting that, so far as it is possible to see, every route of escape is a mirage. But knowing full well what they are, he embraces man's illusions anyway, because he regards the need for illusions as a sufficient truth in itself. At the end of the essay, a "young mortal enters the hall of the firmament," and the gods bless him and beckon him. "On the instant, and incessantly, fall snow-storms of illusions." The young man finds himself in a "mad crowd" which tosses him about and orders him a-round; he feels abandoned and powerless.

> Every moment new changes and new showers of deceptions to baffle and distract him. And when, by and by, for an instant, the air clears and the cloud lifts a little, there are the gods still sitting around him on their thrones, — they alone with him alone. (p. 325)

Is the crowd an illusion, or are the gods? If a rare vision of the firmament enables him to endure his existence in the crowd, then so long as he survives there is no purpose in asking what is real. "I am very easy in my mind," Emerson wrote Carlyle in 1841, "and never dream of suicide. My whole philosophy — which is very real — teaches acquiescence and optimism" (L, p. 304).

In his letter on *The Conduct of Life*, Carlyle was ecstatic over the "finale of all, that of 'Illusions' falling on us like snow-showers, but again of 'the gods sitting stedfast on their thrones' all the while" (p. 534). Carlyle's tragedy was that he was incapable of accepting his own illusions with a sincere, lasting belief, and he resented the illusions of others. Perhaps he had finally learned from Emerson to recognize, if not to accept, the persistence of illusion as a permanent human trait.

Carlyle remained "interesting" to Nietzsche because of his worst quality: his "constant passionate dishonesty against himself." Not that he really lied to himself or to anyone else; on the contrary, it was actually his sincerity that revealed his dishonesty. He could not rest content with the things he wanted to *believe*—an eternal realm of the spirit, the heaven-inspired hero, a society of saints—unless he was certain that they were absolutely *true,* and inevitably his beliefs would collide with realities, particularly with the reality of the finitude of life. He would not accept his beliefs as beliefs, as necessary illusions. When the illusions burst, he would take refuge in silence, or in bombast, or in despair. He could utter the most outrageous opinions, as though he had the freedom to establish as truth whatever he wanted to believe merely by asserting it at the top of his voice. But his demand for belief could never permanently overcome his will to truth; ultimately his faith would always collapse. In this he was only human, all too human. Nietzsche in some sense, and Matthew Arnold to a much greater extent, saw reflected in him their own fear and weakness: hence much of their repulsion. In Carlyle it is possible to read a grim, unflattering representation of self-deluded humanity, as he thrashes about willfully but helplessly against his own limitations. Largely because of his unfailing humor—his instinctive playfulness—and his courage, the vivid self-portrait attracts us, but with a terrible fascination; no wonder so many turn away from Carlyle in disgust, as from a madman.

Emerson does not lie to us either, but he permits us to lie to ourselves, if we wish. Those who feel they can survive in the angry crowd without a glimpse of the firmament are free to try, but the necessity which opposes them is determined by the human condition: they will share the fate of Carlyle. Emerson encourages us to be happy, not with beliefs that are true, but through his gentle madness, his "clever cheerfulness which discourages all seriousness." We turn to him as to an amiable lunatic who seems to tell us whatever it is we think we want to hear.

In attempting to explain themselves to each other, Carlyle

and Emerson reveal themselves to us all. They do even more for us. The one forces us to admit the truth, the other allows us to entertain the illusions which make the truth endurable. Together they help us to look at ourselves with compassion and understanding.

Chronology
Notes
Index

Chronology

Carlyle	Emerson
1795 Born in Ecclefechan, Scotland	
	1803 Born in Boston, Massachusetts
1809-14 Attends Edinburgh University	1811 Death of father
1814-20 Abandons plans to enter ministry, studies law, tutors, teaches school	
	1821 Graduates Harvard College
	1821-24 Teaches at a girls' school
1822 (21?) Leith Walk "conversion" (described in "Everlasting No")	
1824 Translates Goethe, visits London, Paris	
1825 *Life of Schiller*	1825 Begins training for ministry
1826 Marries Jane Welsh	
1828 Moves to Craigenputtock	
1829-31 "Signs of the Times," "Novalis," "Characteristics"; *Sartor Resartus* completed	1829 Ordained as Unitarian minister; marries Ellen Tucker
	1831-32 Death of Ellen; resigns from Second Church
1832 Death of father	1832-33 Travels to Europe, meets Landor, Coleridge, Carlyle
1833 Meets Emerson, August 25	

Carlyle	Emerson
1833-34 *Sartor* appears in *Fraser's Magazine*; moves to London	1833-34 Lectures on "Natural History"; moves to Concord
	1835 Marries Lydia ("Lidian") Jackson
1836 American edition of *Sartor* (first English edition 1838)	1836 *Nature*
1837 *The French Revolution*	1836-37 Lectures on "The Philosophy of History"
1837-40 Lectures on "German Literature," "History of Literature," "Revolutions of Modern Europe," "Heroes and Hero-Worship" (pub. 1841)	1837 "The American Scholar"
	1838 The Divinity School Address
1839 *Chartism*	1839-40 Lectures on "The Present Age"
	1841 Lecture on "Man the Reformer"; *Essays*
1843 *Past and Present*	1842 Death of son Waldo
1844 Death of John Sterling	1844 "The Young American"; address on "Emancipation in the British West Indies"; *Essays, Second Series*
1845 *Oliver Cromwell's Letters and Speeches*	1845-46 Lectures on "Representative Men" (pub. 1850); *Poems*
1848 Visits Stonehenge with Emerson	1847-48 Lecture tour in Britain; visits France
1849 "Nigger Question"	
1850 *Latter-Day Pamphlets*	1850 Death of Margaret Fuller
1851 *Life of John Sterling*	1851-52 Lectures on "The Conduct of Life" (pub. 1860)
1852-65 *Frederick the Great*, in six volumes (pub. 1859-65)	1852 *Memoirs of Margaret Fuller Ossoli*
	1856 *English Traits*
	1858 Meets John Brown
	1862 Address on "Thoreau"
1866 Death of Jane Carlyle; Eyre Controversy	
1867 "Shooting Niagara"	
1872-73 Sees Emerson	1872-73 House burns; travels in Britain, Europe, and Near East
1881 Dies; buried in Ecclefechan	1881 Address on "Carlyle"
	1882 Dies; buried in Concord

Notes

For a Carlyle-Emerson bibliography, see *The Correspondence of Carlyle and Emerson*, ed. Joseph Slater (New York, 1964), pp. 591-601. For further research on Carlyle, see G. B. Tennyson, "The Carlyles" in *Victorian Prose: A Guide to Research*, ed. David J. DeLaura (New York, 1973), pp. 31-111. There is no complete bibliography of Emerson. For a selected bibliography, see *Emerson: A Collection of Critical Essays*, ed. Milton R. Konvitz and Stephen E. Whicher (Englewood Cliffs, N.J., 1962); see also the annual volumes of *American Literary Scholarship*, ed. J. A. Robbins (Durham, N.C., 1963-).

INTRODUCTION

1. Henry James, Jr., "The Correspondence of Carlyle and Emerson," *The Century Magazine*, 26 (June 1883), 271. It should be added that James also said that "the temperament of the one was absolutely opposed to the temperament of the other" (p. 269).

2. Ralph L. Rusk, *The Life of Ralph Waldo Emerson* (New York, 1949), pp. 115-128; Charles Eliot Norton, *Letters*, ed. Sara Norton and M. A. DeWolfe Howe (Boston, 1913), I, 504; James Anthony Froude, *My Relations with Carlyle* (New York, 1903), p. 7.

3. Compare EW 10:456, 458, 479 ("Thoreau") with EW 10:491-494 ("Carlyle"). Also cf. Joel Porte, *Emerson and Thoreau: Transcendentalists in Conflict* (Middletown, Conn., 1965), p. 195.

4. Moncure D. Conway, "Thomas Carlyle," *Harper's New Monthly Magazine*, 62 (1881), 899. Also cf. L, p. 12.

5. For Emerson, see Henry F. Pommer, *Emerson's First Marriage* (Carbondale, Ill., 1967). For Carlyle, see the beautiful lament he wrote for his father in 1832, published posthumously in *Reminiscences*, ed. J. A. Froude (New York, 1881), pp. 3-33.

6. For a widely accepted analysis of the Leith Walk episode cf. Carlisle Moore, "*Sartor Resartus* and the Problem of Carlyle's Conversion," *PMLA*, 70 (1955), 662-681. For the theme of death in Emerson, see Jonathan Bishop, *Emerson on the Soul* (Cambridge, Mass., 1964), pp. 171, 178-179.

7. Ernest Becker, *Escape from Evil* (New York, 1975), p. 64; and see his previous book, *The Denial of Death* (New York, 1973).

8. Cf. the "Translator's Preface" (1929) in Immanuel Kant, *Critique of Pure Reason*, trans. Norman Kemp Smith (New York, 1965), pp. vi-vii.

9. For Carlyle, see Charles Frederick Harrold, *Carlyle and German Thought: 1819-1834* (New Haven, Conn., 1934). Also useful is an earlier study by Margaret Storrs, *The Relation of Carlyle to Kant and Fichte* (Bryn Mawr, Pa., 1929). For Emerson, see Kenneth W. Cameron, *Emerson the Essayist*, 2 vols. (Raleigh, N.C., 1945); and Merton M. Sealts, Jr., and Alfred R. Ferguson, eds., *Emerson's Nature: Origin, Growth, Meaning* (New York, 1969). René Wellek has studied the influence of German philosophy on both writers; see the excellent articles reprinted in his *Confrontations* (Princeton, N.J., 1965).

1. The Transatlantic Transcendentalists

1. The journal entry reads: "Every event affects all the future e.g. Christ died on the tree, that built Dunscore Church yonder & always affects us two. The merely relative existence of Time & hence his faith in his immortality." Emerson, *Journals and Miscellaneous Notebooks*, ed. Gilman et. al. (Cambridge, Mass., 1960-), IV, 220-221.

2. Emerson, *Letters*, ed. Ralph L. Rusk (New York, 1939), I, 394.

3. That much had appeared by March; Emerson's letter is dated 14 May 1834. Emerson subscribed to *Fraser's* before leaving England and wrote to Fraser from Boston encouraging him to continue the serialization. Cf. L, pp. 16, 98n.

4. E. M. W. Tillyard, *Milton* (1930; paperback ed., New York, 1967), pp. 188-189. I have expanded the idea somewhat without, I hope, violating Tillyard's meaning.

5. Lawrence Buell, *Literary Transcendentalism: Style and Vision in the American Renaissance* (Ithaca, N.Y., 1973; paperback ed., 1975), p. 15, and cf. pp. 143-144.

6. Rusk, pp. 235, 243.

7. Carlyle, *Two Notebooks*, ed. Charles Eliot Norton (1898; reprint ed., New York, 1972), p. 151. (The phrases from *Nature* are in *NAL*, pp. 17, 22.)

8. Perry Miller, comp., *The Transcendentalists* (Cambridge, Mass., 1950), pp. 193-194. The more liberal English Unitarians were generally more receptive to Emerson's writings: cf. Clarence Gohdes, *American*

Literature in Nineteenth-Century England (New York, 1944), pp. 146-147; and William J. Sowder, *Emerson's Impact on the British Isles and Canada* (Charlottesville, Va., 1966), pp. 11-12. During his 1847-48 lecture tour in Britain, Emerson encountered some opposition from the Church of England and more from the Swedenborgians: cf. Rusk, p. 333.

9. Arthur C. McGiffert, Jr., comp., *Young Emerson Speaks* (Boston, 1938), p. 42; and cf. "Miracles," pp. 120-126. Also cf. Buell, pp. 118-119.

10. Carlyle, *Two Notebooks*, p. 151.

11. Charles Gavan Duffy, *Conversations with Carlyle* (New York, 1892), p. 93.

12. G. B. Tennyson, *Sartor Called Resartus* (Princeton, N.J., 1965), p. 280.

13. Ibid., pp. 254-257.

14. Ibid., p. 230.

15. Tennyson, p. 258. A likely source of Carlyle's rhetorical strategy is a section from Novalis's *Lehrlinge zu Sais* entitled "Nature," part of which Carlyle translated in the "Novalis" essay. Death is (partly) the subject, and among the "speakers" are "a more courageous Class," "Several," and "an earnest Man." Cf. CW 27:32-35.

16. Tennyson, pp. 304-312. Another possible source may be a passage from Schiller's novel *Der Geisterseher* which Carlyle translated in his *Life of Schiller*; cf. CW 25:50-51.

17. Harrold's comments, along with the substance of Sterling's letter and Carlyle's reply (first published in Carlyle's *Life of Sterling*), are in SR, pp. 305-318. Sterling never made his reservations public and rarely repeated them even to close friends, though in an 1840 letter to Richard Trench he described *Sartor Resartus* as "in the main a litany of despair"; cf. Anne Tuell, *John Sterling: A Representative Victorian* (New York, 1941), p. 313.

18. James Anthony Froude, *Thomas Carlyle: A History of the First Forty Years of His Life* (New York, 1882), II, 7-13.

19. Duffy, p. 93.

20. The journal entry is in Emerson, *Journals and Miscellaneous Notebooks*, V, 111-112. The editor, Merton M. Sealts, Jr., also believes that the entry refers to "Natural Supernaturalism." For more on the conception and composition of *Nature* see Sealts and Ferguson, *Emerson's Nature*.

21. James Elliot Cabot, *A Memoir of Ralph Waldo Emerson* (Boston, 1888), I, 241.

22. *Sartor Resartus, In Three Books* (Boston, 1836), pp. iii-iv. Harrold includes Carlyle's almost identical 1838 reprint of the preface in SR, pp. 324-325.

23. Emerson, *Journals and Miscellaneous Notebooks*, V, 408.

2. SELF-DENIAL AND SELF-RELIANCE

1. For more on "Bibliopoly" see L, pp. 16-29. In the letter, Slater provides the missing "tat"; I omitted Slater's brackets.

2. *Essays* by R. W. Emerson with Preface by Thomas Carlyle (London, 1841), pp. vi-xii. A small part of Carlyle's preface is reprinted in Milton R. Konvitz, ed., *The Recognition of Ralph Waldo Emerson* (Ann Arbor, Mich., 1972), p. 19.

3. See the Introduction to Emerson, *Early Lectures*, ed. Stephen E. Whicher and Robert E. Spiller (Cambridge, Mass., 1959), I, xii-xxvii. A few of the lectures, such as "Man the Reformer" (1841) and three of the "Lectures on the Times" (1841-42), were published in *The Dial*, but after dismissing the first number as "*too* ethereal, speculative, and theoretic" (L, p. 280) and praising only Emerson's "Thoughts on Modern Literature" in the second, Carlyle rarely mentioned the journal again and probably seldom bothered reading it.

4. Emerson, *Letters*, I, 395.

5. Richard Monckton Milnes, "American Philosophy—Emerson's Works," *London and Westminster Review*, 33 (1840), 345. Reprinted in part in *Recognition of Emerson*, pp. 16-18.

6. For "Calvinist without the theology" see Froude, *First Forty Years*, II, 1-7. Carlyle rarely went to any kind of church in London; cf. James Anthony Froude, *Thomas Carlyle: A History of His Life in London* (New York, 1884), I, 37. In *Life in London*, II, 385ff., Froude tells of the aged Carlyle attending services at St. Paul's for the first time and almost causing a scene during the sermon. In his *Puritan Temper and Transcendental Faith: Carlyle's Literary Vision* (Columbus, Ohio, 1972), pp. 120-121 and passim, A. Abbott Ikeler uses the Froude phrase along with "Calvinist prejudices," etc., and cites others who have expressed similar views.

7. The most brilliant consideration of Emerson's "Puritanism" is Perry Miller's controversial article, "From Edwards to Emerson," *New England Quarterly*, 12 (1940), 587-617. Frederick B. Wahr in *Emerson and Goethe* (1915; reprint ed., Hartford, Conn., 1971), pp. 38-39, said Emerson had "the roots of his thought firmly embedded in the ethical tradition of Puritanic Calvinism." In his recent *The Puritan Origins of the American Self* (New Haven, Conn., 1975), pp. 166-167, Sacvan Bercovitch describes Emerson's admiration for the colonial Puritans. Also cf. Paul K. Conkin, *Puritans and Pragmatists: Eight Eminent American Thinkers* (1968; paperback ed., Bloomington, Ind., 1976), pp. 163-165.

8. Cf. Harrold, *Carlyle and German Thought*, pp. 206-208, 214-230.

9. CW 11:130-131. More of the letter is in Julius Hare's Memoir of Sterling in John Sterling, *Essays and Tales* (London, 1848), I, lxxiv. Hare did not identify "B."; Carlyle himself clarified it in his *Life of Sterling*. It is also possible that Carlyle was holding back on his memory of private

discussions with Sterling on religion to avoid reviving the public controversy regarding Sterling's orthodoxy that erupted in response to Hare's *Memoir*. See the chapter, "Sterling and the Religious Newspapers" in Tuell's book, pp. 351-371.

10. Cf. Philip Rosenberg, *The Seventh Hero: Thomas Carlyle and the Theory of Radical Activism* (Cambridge, Mass., 1974), pp. 60-62.

11. In *Emerson on the Soul*, Bishop relates this passage and another, similar passage in *Representative Men* to a dream Emerson recorded in his journal; cf. Bishop, pp. 41-43.

12. Stephen E. Whicher, *Freedom and Fate: An Inner Life of Ralph Waldo Emerson* (Philadelphia, Pa., 1953), pp. 124, 139. Also cf. Conkin, pp. 163-164.

13. Cf. Whicher, p. 57.

14. Henry David Thoreau, "Thomas Carlyle" in *Works* (Walden ed.), IV, 345-346.

15. Rosenberg, p. 193.

16. Cf. Rosenberg, pp. 200-203. Although Rosenberg's provocative book has greatly influenced my conception of Carlyle, I disagree with much of what he says and accept some of his conclusions for very different reasons from his. He insists, for example, that Carlyle's heroes are totally determined: cf. pp. 188-193. I think Rosenberg was overreacting to Sidney Hook, who preferred the opposite extreme. I find myself somewhere on the Hook-side of the middle.

17. For the intellectual background of Emerson's "representative" idea, see John O. McCormick, "Emerson's Theory of Human Greatness," *New England Quarterly*, 26 (1953), 291-314. McCormick sees Hegel as Emerson's ultimate source via Cousin, but he is also aware of the Swedenborgian influences that F. O. Matthiessen takes up in his *American Renaissance*. Also cf. Émile Montégut, "Du Culte des Héroes: Carlyle et Emerson," *Revue des Deux Mondes*, 7 (1850), 722-737, and especially p. 728. Some of what I say resembles the ideas in this fascinating contemporary comparison of Carlyle and Emerson.

18. Rusk, pp. 164-165.

19. Emerson, *Early Lectures*, I, 136.

20. Froude, *First Forty Years*, II, 80. For Sterling's article see Sterling, *Essays and Tales*, I, 374-381.

21. Rusk, p. 503.

22. Emerson, *Journals and Miscellaneous Notebooks*, IV, 192; Emerson, *Journals*, ed. Edward Waldo Emerson and Waldo Emerson Forbes (Boston, 1909-14), VIII, 249. For the *Representative Men* passages, cf. EW 4:270, 289. And cf. Wahr, pp. 26-27.

23. *Correspondence between Goethe and Carlyle*, ed. Charles Eliot Norton (London, 1887), p. 7 ("Disciple to his Master"); p. 226 (Saint-

Simonians); pp. 164, 182 (Utilitarians); pp. 80-81 (letter to John Carlyle). The immediate provocation of the letter to John was Carlyle's displeasure with the company he had learned Goethe was keeping.

24. Ibid., p. 2.

25. Froude, *First Forty Years*, I, 240; cf. I, chap. 7.

26. *Goethe-Carlyle Correspondence*, pp. 283-284. In his *Puritan Temper*, Ikeler covers some of this same ground, but from the angle of esthetics; cf. pp. 27-29.

27. This is the thrust of Ikeler's book, although he sees a continuing tension between the two "tendencies" throughout Carlyle's life. Ikeler's first chapter, "Carlyle on Literature: Conflicting Views," is a good summary of the problem and includes (pp. 10-11) some examples of similar observations by other critics.

28. Froude, *First Forty Years*, II, 80.

29. A. O. J. Cockshut, *Truth to Life: The Art of Biography in the Nineteenth Century* (1974; paperback ed., New York, 1976), p. 195.

30. It might be objected that, since German literature was still not widely known in England, Carlyle's choices for the Hero as Man of Letters were made primarily for the benefit of his English listeners, for whom Goethe might have been too unfamiliar. But Carlyle's lecture series on "The History of Literature," delivered two years earlier in the same hall, had ended with a lecture on "modern German literature," dealing mainly with Goethe, Schiller, and Richter. This series survives in the form of notes taken by a subscriber, Thomas Anstey. I have not discussed Anstey's notes because of their secondhand nature and because in most matters that interest me, such as the question of Goethe, Anstey's reports add almost nothing to what Carlyle himself published elsewhere. Cf. Thomas Carlyle, *Lectures on the History of Literature*, ed. J. Reay Greene (New York, 1892), pp. 214-218. He also spoke on Goethe in 1837.

31. Rusk, pp. 106-108. Also cf. E. W. Emerson's note in EW 4:366-368.

32. Cockshut, p. 12. Even on its own terms, Carlyle's methods may work only in short pieces like the hero lectures and not in sustained, full-length biographies. That might help explain Carlyle's inability to produce a life of Cromwell and the morass he slowly sank into with *Frederick the Great*. The earlier *Life of Schiller* and, as shall be seen, the *Life of Sterling* were written in a different manner. *Sartor Resartus*, as fictionalized autobiography, and the *Reminiscences*, also autobiographical, are different cases entirely.

33. The best literary study is the chapter entitled "Limited Heroism: *John Sterling*" in Albert J. LaValley, *Carlyle and the Idea of the Modern* (New Haven, Conn., 1968), pp. 303-327. Tuell's book is also useful. It is a pity that Cockshut does not take up the book, except for an occasional

passing reference, since many of his insights into nineteenth-century biography are applicable to it. But the omission was probably inevitable and even desirable in view of Cockshut's grossly unfair conception of Carlyle as a man who "despised almost everything and everybody, except his parents and Oliver Cromwell" (p. 148).

34. R. W. Emerson, W. H. Channing, and J. F. Clarke, *Memoirs of Margaret Fuller Ossoli* (1852; reprint ed., New York, 1972), I, 228.

35. The *Memoirs*, of course, was a collective enterprise to which Emerson contributed a segment. Emerson admired the *Life of Sterling*, especially the quality of the writing; "This living narration," he wrote in his journal, "is daguerreotyped in his page." But, he added, Carlyle did not "very much uncover his secret mind" (*Journals*, VIII, 261-262). For his relation to Sterling, see *The Correspondence of Emerson and Sterling*, ed. E. W. Emerson (Boston, 1897); and, of course, cf. the frequent mention of Sterling in L.

3. PAST AND PRESENT

1. Cf. L, pp. 35-36. The section of Joseph Slater's Introduction entitled "Interlude 1847-1848" comprises a concise but complete summary of virtually all the documentation concerning the Emerson-Carlyle relationship during Emerson's trip. It may be assumed that any quotation for which I fail to identify the source may be found in that section. My interpretations are my own and sometimes differ from Slater's.

2. Emerson, *Letters*, III, 424; and cf. p. 438.

3. Jane Welsh Carlyle, *Letters and Memorials*, ed. J. A. Froude (New York, 1883), I, 205. Also cf. a letter written about the same time from Carlyle to his brother Alexander, who had recently emigrated to Canada, describing Yankees, with "some few shining exceptions," as "truly unpleasant," "full of cant, full of vanity," and so on. Thomas Carlyle, *Letters to His Brother Alexander*, ed. Edwin W. Marrs, Jr. (Cambridge, Mass., 1968), p. 579.

4. A. Bronson Alcott, *Letters*, ed. Richard L. Herrnstadt (Cedar Falls, Iowa, 1969), pp. 78-79. Also cf. E. P. Whipple, "Emerson and Carlyle," *The North American Review*, 136 (1883), 439: "It was rumored at the time that [Alcott] wrote to Emerson in these words: 'I accuse T. Carlyle of inhospitality to my thought'."

5. Emerson, *Letters*, IV, 31.

6. Duffy, p. 94.

7. Excerpted in Iris Origo, "The Carlyles and the Ashburtons," *The Cornhill Magazine*, 164 (1949-50), 462.

8. *Marx & Engels: Basic Writings on Politics and Philosophy*, ed. Lewis S. Feuer (New York, 1959), p. 9.

9. In his excellent study, *Engels, Manchester, and the Working Class*

(New York, 1974), pp. 102-112, Steven Marcus explores Engels's early attitude toward Carlyle, which he feels virtually amounted to identification.

10. George Fitzhugh, *Cannibals All! or Slaves Without Masters*, ed. C. Vann Woodward (Cambridge, Mass., 1960), p. 32.

11. Georg Lukács, *The Theory of the Novel* (Cambridge, Mass., 1971), p. 19.

12. Friedrich Engels, *The Condition of the Working Class in England*, ed. W. O. Henderson and W. H. Chaloner (Palo Alto, Calif., 1958), p. 331n.

13. G. B. Tennyson, "The Carlyles" in *Victorian Prose: A Guide to Research*, ed. David J. DeLaura (New York, 1973), pp. 47, 57.

14. Carlyle, *Reminiscences*, pp. 77-78.

15. Carlyle, *Letters to His Brother*, pp. 30-31.

16. Ibid., p. 772.

17. René Wellek, "Carlyle and the Philosophy of History" in *Confrontations*, pp. 87-88. For a concise summary of Victorian approaches to history, see Jerome H. Buckley, *The Triumph of Time* (Cambridge, Mass., 1966), especially chap. 2, "The Uses of History," pp. 14-33.

18. Sterling, *Essays and Tales*, I, 366. Also anent Carlyle's pyrophilia: he wrote in his *Reminiscences* (pp. 90-91) that he could not forget a grisly anecdote he heard from his father about a mad woman who burned to death in a furnace.

19. Rosenberg, pp. 103-104.

20. Sterling, I, 372.

21. Rosenberg, pp. 22-23.

22. Cf. Rosenberg, pp. 193-200.

23. Harrold, p. 176. Also cf. Thomas Carlyle, *Two Reminiscences*, ed. John Clubbe (Durham, N.C., 1974), pp. 98-99.

24. Cf. Herbert L. Sussman, *Victorians and the Machine* (Cambridge, Mass., 1968), pp. 25-26, for a "Calvinist" interpretation.

25. Part of the drillmaster idea may have been suggested to Carlyle by his research on Prussian pedagogy for *Frederick the Great*: cf. CW 12:423-426.

26. Sterling, I, 274-275.

27. Carlyle, *Letters to His Brother*, pp. 545-546.

28. Engels, pp. 113-114.

29. He also favored universal education, certainly a progressive idea. But the point is that he never proposed or initiated specific actions to realize this goal or any other.

30. Emerson, *Letters*, III, 424.

31. Rusk, pp. 68, 96.

32. Emerson, *Journals and Miscellaneous Notebooks*, III, 229.

33. Walter E. Houghton, *The Victorian Frame of Mind* (New Haven, Conn., 1957), p. 3.

34. Leo Marx, *The Machine in the Garden* (New York, 1964), p. 231.

35. Rusk, pp. 292, 299.

36. Emerson, *Letters*, III, 461. And cf. Phyllis Cole, "Emerson, England, and Fate" in *Emerson: Prophecy, Metamorphosis, and Influence*, ed. David Levin (New York, 1975), pp. 85-86.

37. Emerson, *Letters*, IV, 35.

38. Rusk, pp. 341-352.

39. "Mind & Manners of the XIX century"; Houghton Library mss., Lectures and Sermons of Ralph Waldo Emerson, 200(8), leaves 49, 50.

40. Cole, p. 98.

41. Cf. Philip L. Nicoloff, *Emerson on Race and History: An Examination of English Traits* (New York, 1961), pp. 118-126, 158, and passim.

42. Ibid., p. 236.

43. Cf. *ET*, p. xv, and Nicoloff, p. 35. I dissent from Jones's distaste for chapter I. I admit it is not indispensable as part of this particular book, but I like it for itself.

44. *The Education of Henry Adams* (Boston, 1961), p. 125. Also cf. Rusk, p. 334.

45. Nicoloff, p. 35.

46. Ibid., p. 152. Nicoloff shows that Emerson does much more with the myth than is mentioned here; cf. pp. 142-174 and passim. Especially interesting is his identification of a "closeted skeleton" in the book, that the Saxon race in America may have been deteriorating (p. 144).

47. Cole, p. 96.

48. Houghton Library ms., 202(2), leaf marked 55 in pencil in lower left-hand corner.

49. Ibid., leaf marked 73 in lower left-hand corner.

50. Cf. Leo Marx's long note on p. 262.

51. Cf. Daniel Aaron, *The Unwritten War* (New York, 1973), pp. 34-38.

52. Emerson, *Letters*, IV, 86.

53. Daniel Aaron, *Men of Good Hope* (New York, 1951), pp. 10-11.

54. Cf. Nicoloff, pp. 111-118; Whicher, *Freedom and Fate*, pp. 141-148; and Jeffrey L. Duncan, *The Power and Form of Emerson's Thought* (Charlottesville, Va., 1973), pp. 11-15, 20-23. Nicoloff nevertheless sees Emerson's conception of history as essentially "pessimistic," even in comparison with Carlyle; cf. pp. 82-83.

55. Cabot, *Memoir of Emerson*, II, 428-430: "The brute instinct rallies and centres in the black man. He is created on a lower plane than the white, and eats men, and kidnaps and tortures if he can." This is from Emerson's 1837 speech at Concord.

56. Cf. Marjory M. Moody, "The Evolution of Emerson as an Abolitionist," *American Literature*, 17 (1945), 8-9.

57. Emery Neff, *Carlyle and Mill* (New York, 1926), pp. 40-43. They

met for the last time in 1846 (p. 37).

58. Cf. Gerald M. Straka, "The Spirit of Carlyle in the Old South," *The Historian*, 20 (1957), 39-57.

59. Sowder, p. 168.

60. Moncure D. Conway, *Thomas Carlyle* (New York, 1881), pp. 95-100. However, Emerson himself questioned Conway's veracity in a letter to Carlyle (L, p. 586). Furthermore, in 1865 Carlyle considered writing a pamphlet in defense of the imprisoned Jefferson Davis; cf. *Reminiscences*, p. 309.

61. Gillian Workman, "Thomas Carlyle and the Governor Eyre Controversy," *Victorian Studies*, 18 (1974), 81.

62. Cf. Nicoloff, pp. 267-268.

63. Also cf. Emerson, *Letters to a Friend 1838-1853*, ed. Charles Eliot Norton (Boston, 1899), pp. 73-75.

Conclusion

1. Horatio Nelson Powers, "A Day with Emerson," *Lippincott's Monthly Magazine*, 30 (1882), 479.

2. Cf. Slater's Introduction, L, pp. 80-81.

3. L, p. 540; and cf. Emerson, *Journals*, X, 51, for a similar sentiment.

4. "The Correspondence of Carlyle and Emerson," *The Spectator*, 56 (1883), 387. Sowder feels that this review "states fairly the final estimate of the two writers in nineteenth-century periodicals."

5. Rusk, p. 473.

6. See Sowder, pp. 184-215, for a good account of the relationship as seen by British periodicals.

7. James Russell Lowell, *A Fable for Critics* (Boston, 1848), p. 45.

8. Sowder, p. 206.

9. Matthew Arnold, *Discourses in America* (London, 1889), p. 167.

10. Arnold, p. vi.

11. Ibid., p. 196.

12. Ibid., p. 166.

13. Moncure D. Conway, *Autobiography* (Boston, 1904), II, 340n.

14. David J. DeLaura, "Arnold and Carlyle," *PMLA*, 79 (1964), 106-107.

15. Arnold, pp. 198-207.

16. For Carlyle and Nietzsche, see Eric Bentley, *A Century of Hero-Worship* (Philadelphia, 1944); LaValley, *Carlyle and the Idea of the Modern*; Tennyson, *Sartor Called Resartus*.

17. Friedrich Nietzsche, *The Will to Power*, trans. Walter Kaufmann and R. J. Hollingdale (New York, 1968), sec. 455, p. 249 (from his notebook, 1888).

18. Nietzsche, *The Antichrist*, sec. 54, in *The Portable Nietzsche*, trans. Walter Kaufmann (New York, 1954), p. 638.

19. *Portable Nietzsche*, pp. 521-522.

20. It was from a letter to Carlyle's mother (8 November 1847) which Nietzsche read in Froude, *Life in London*, I, 355. Cf. L, pp. 34-35.

21. Stanley Hubbard, *Nietzsche und Emerson* (Basel, 1958), p. 177. I apologize for my translation.

22. Emerson, *Journals and Miscellaneous Notebooks*, X, 542; and cf. *Letters*, IV, 39.

Index

TC = Thomas Carlyle
RWE = Ralph Waldo Emerson